M̶a̶r̶i̶o̶n̶ ...on

Love's Austere and Lonely Offices

Street Portraits and Poems

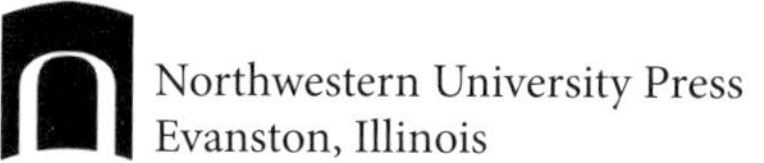

Northwestern University Press
Evanston, Illinois

Northwestern University Press
www.nupress.northwestern.edu

Printed in Canada

10   9   8   7   6   5   4   3   2   1

Library of Congress Cataloging-in-Publication Data

Names: Jackson, Marcus, 1981– author
Title: Love's austere and lonely offices : street portraits and poems / Marcus Jackson.
Description: Evanston : Northwestern University Press, 2026.
Identifiers: LCCN 2026001355 | ISBN 9798899480508 paperback
Subjects: LCSH: Street photography—Ohio—Columbus | Street photography—New York (State)—New York | American poetry—African American authors | American poetry—21st century | BISAC: PHOTOGRAPHY / Subjects & Themes / Street Photography | POETRY / American / African American & Black | LCGFT: Fiction | Photographs | Poetry
Classification: LCC PS3610.A35427 L68 2026
LC record available at https://lccn.loc.gov/2026001355

Contents

I.

Shoeless Acrobatics on High Street

From the old killings, the new killings
differ only slightly, and my grace
is the same as my grandmother's,

a grace originally born on some night
specified by the blue, weighty air,
and by the soil insisting

violence is veiled meagerness.
Certainly, there were landlords,
hungers, nakedness, and taxes

all to be quelled, so I've worked among others,
into exhaustion and trepidation,
though I've somehow retained the fluidity

bequeathed to me, moving
through the city, still struck
with sudden glances of dusk

daubing clouds above the high-rises,
the enormous nervous system
of crosswalks and traffic lights,

the memory of dancing as a child, and today
the great want, as if no faulty flip
or no hateful, mistaken man could kill me,

to still be dancing.

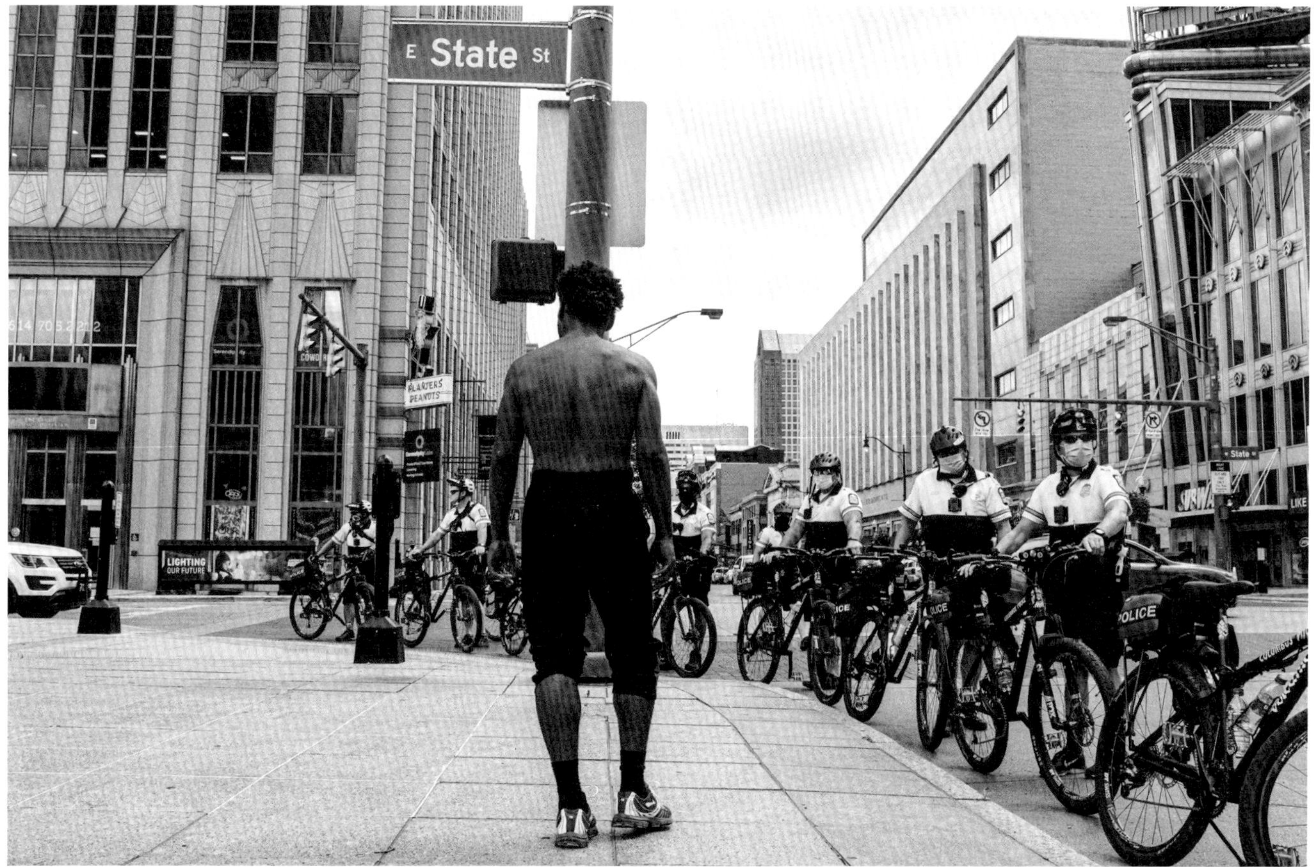E State St
PLANTERS
PEANUTS
LIGHTING
OUR FUTURE
POLICE
POLICE
POLICE

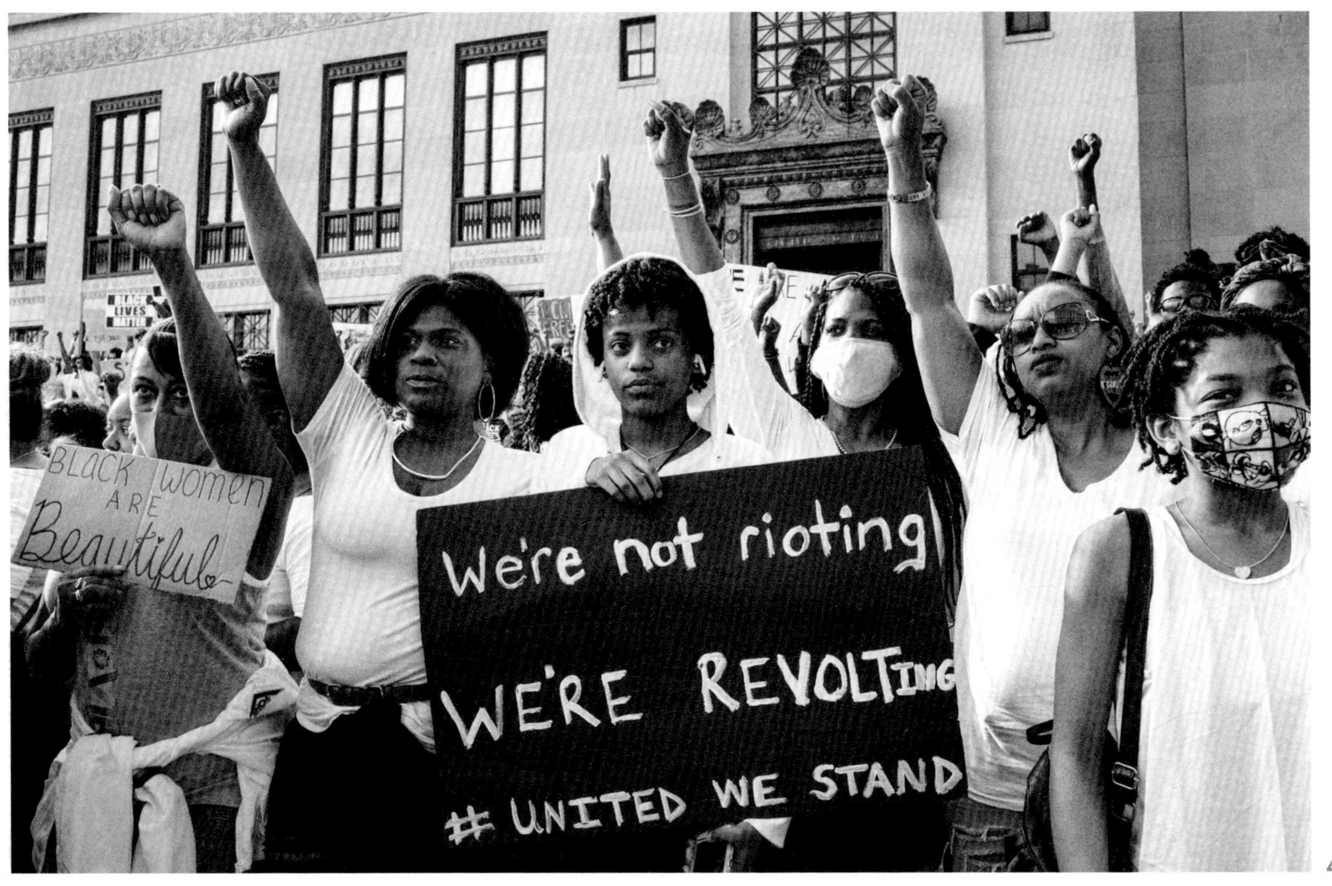

BLACK LIVES MATTER
BLACK WOMEN ARE Beautiful
We're not rioting
WE'RE REVOLTing
UNITED WE STAND

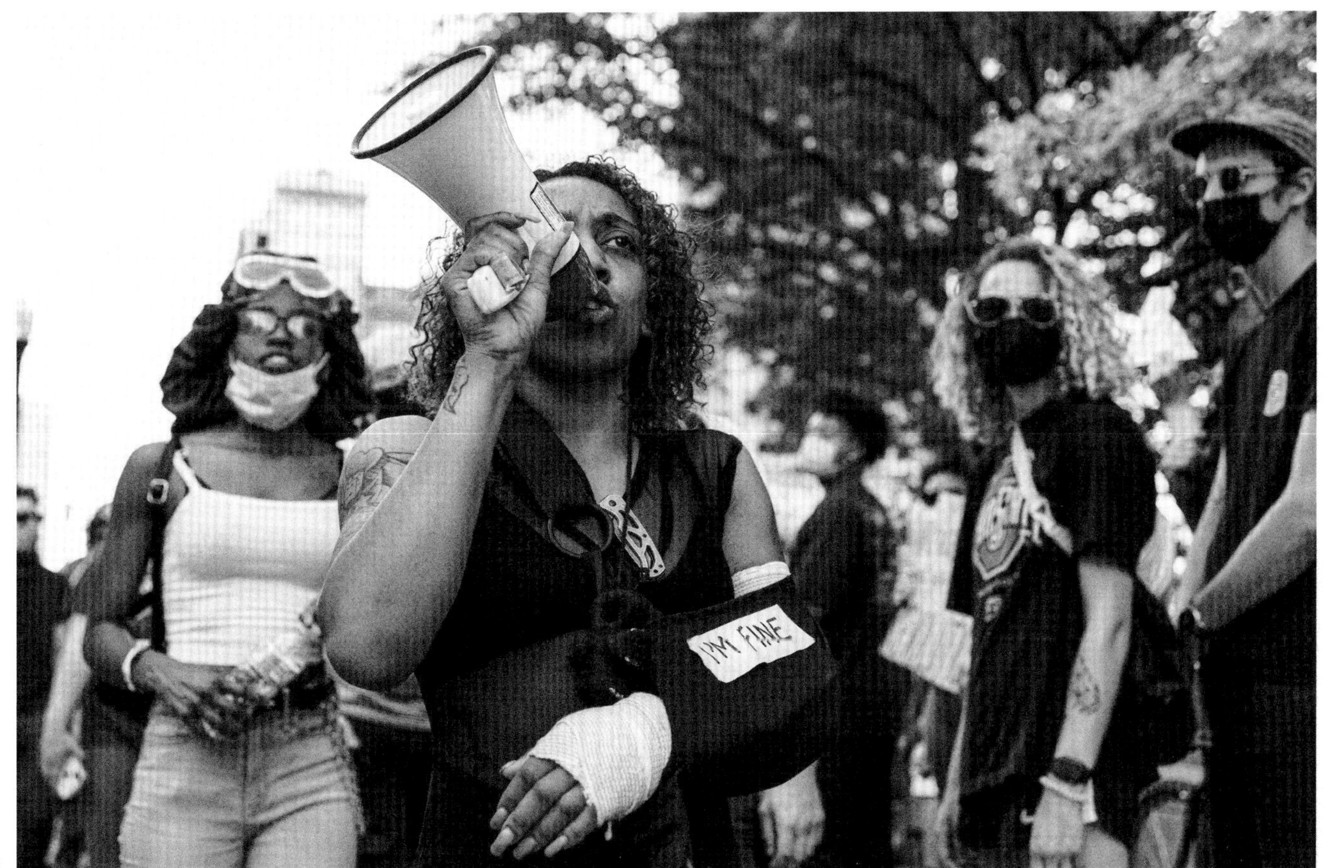
I'M FINE

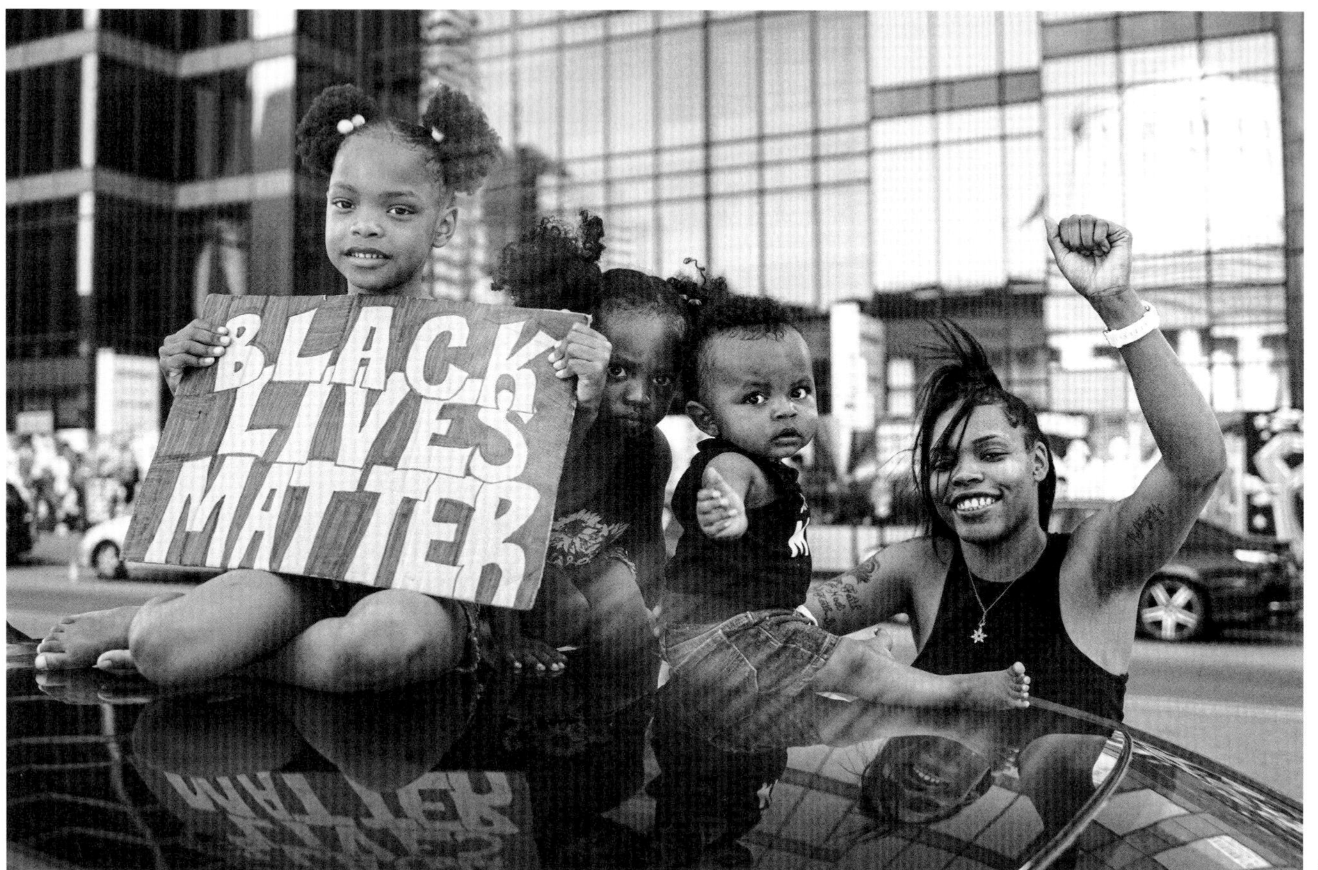

BLACK
LIVES
MATTER

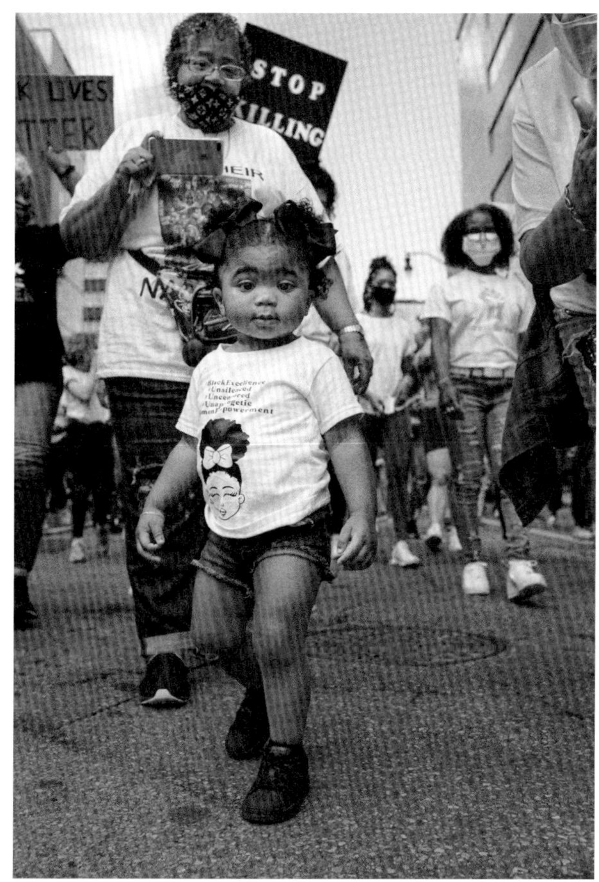
K LIVES
TTER
STOP
KILLING
Black Excellence
Unsilenced
Uncensored
Unapologetic
Empowerment

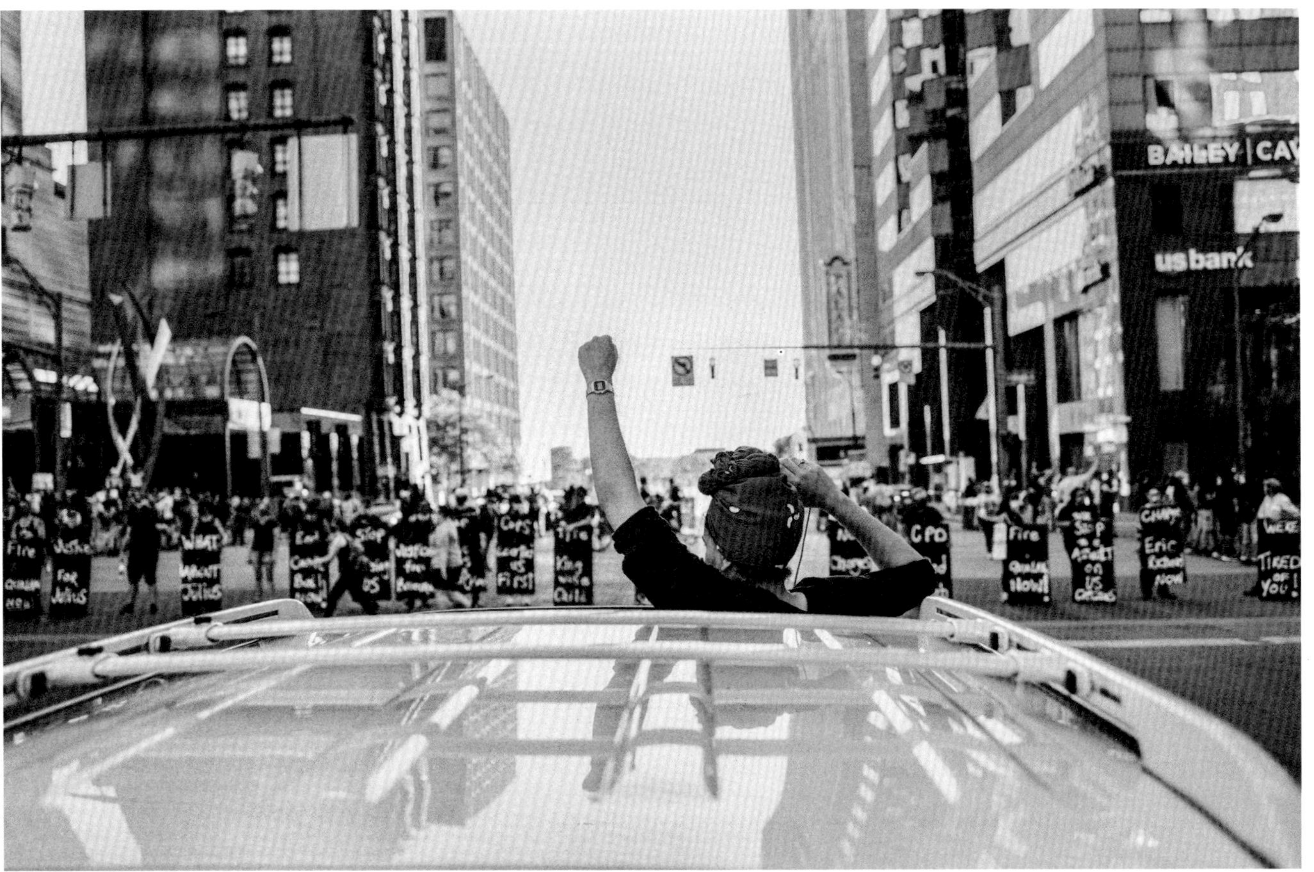

8

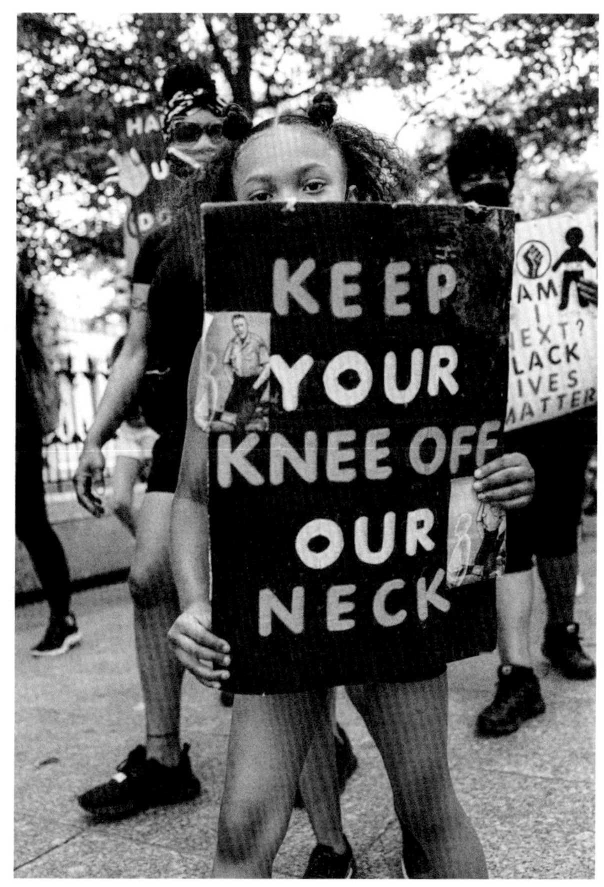
KEEP
YOUR
KNEE OFF
OUR
NECK
AM
I
NEXT?
BLACK
LIVES
MATTER

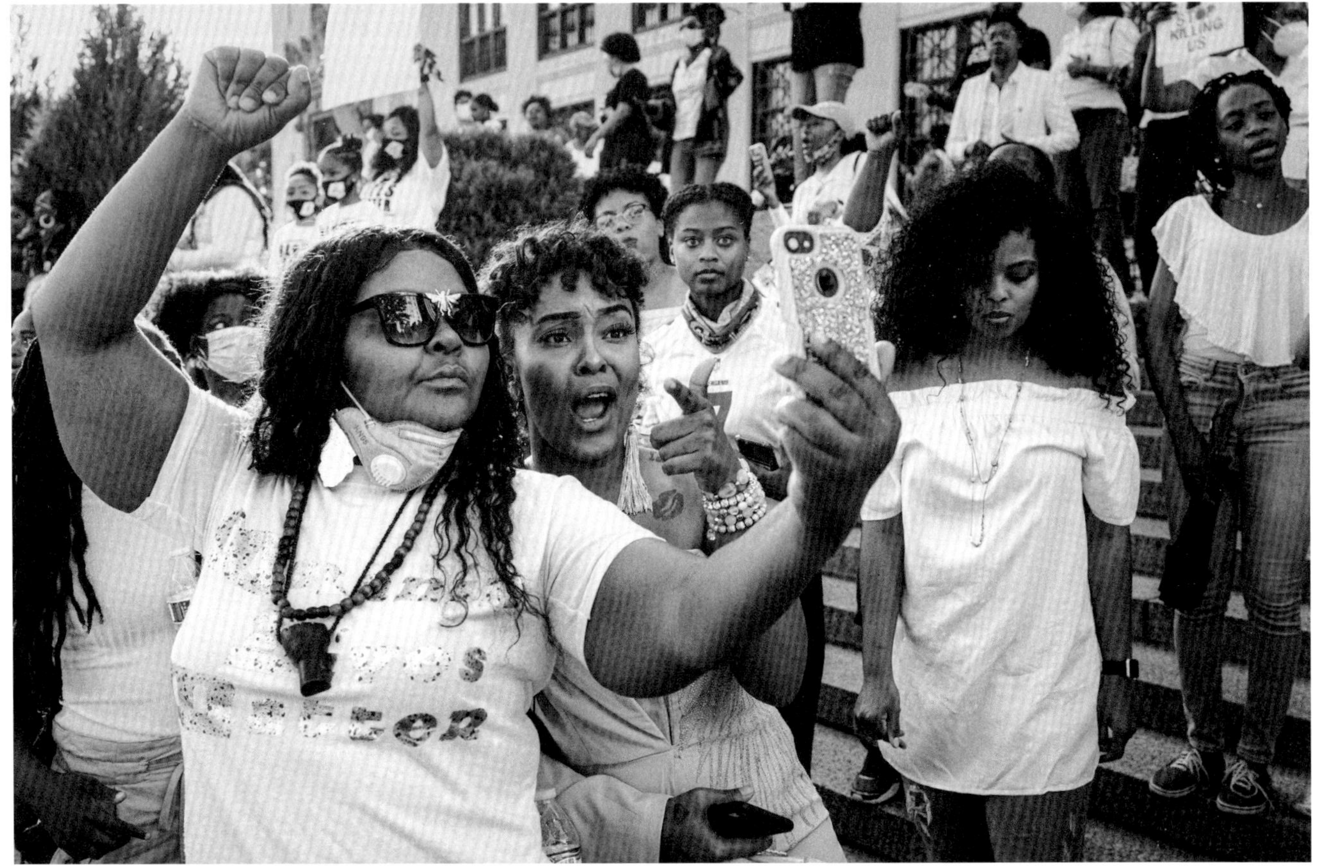

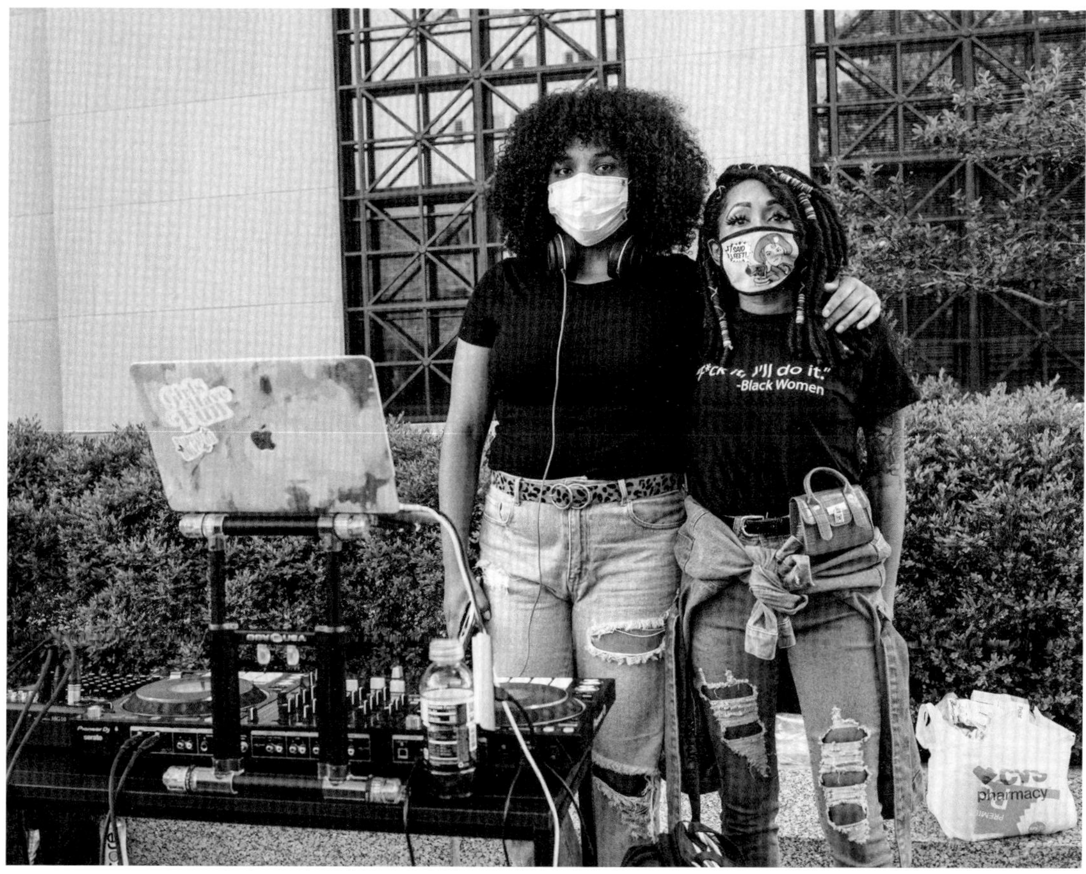
"f*ck it, I'll do it."
-Black Women

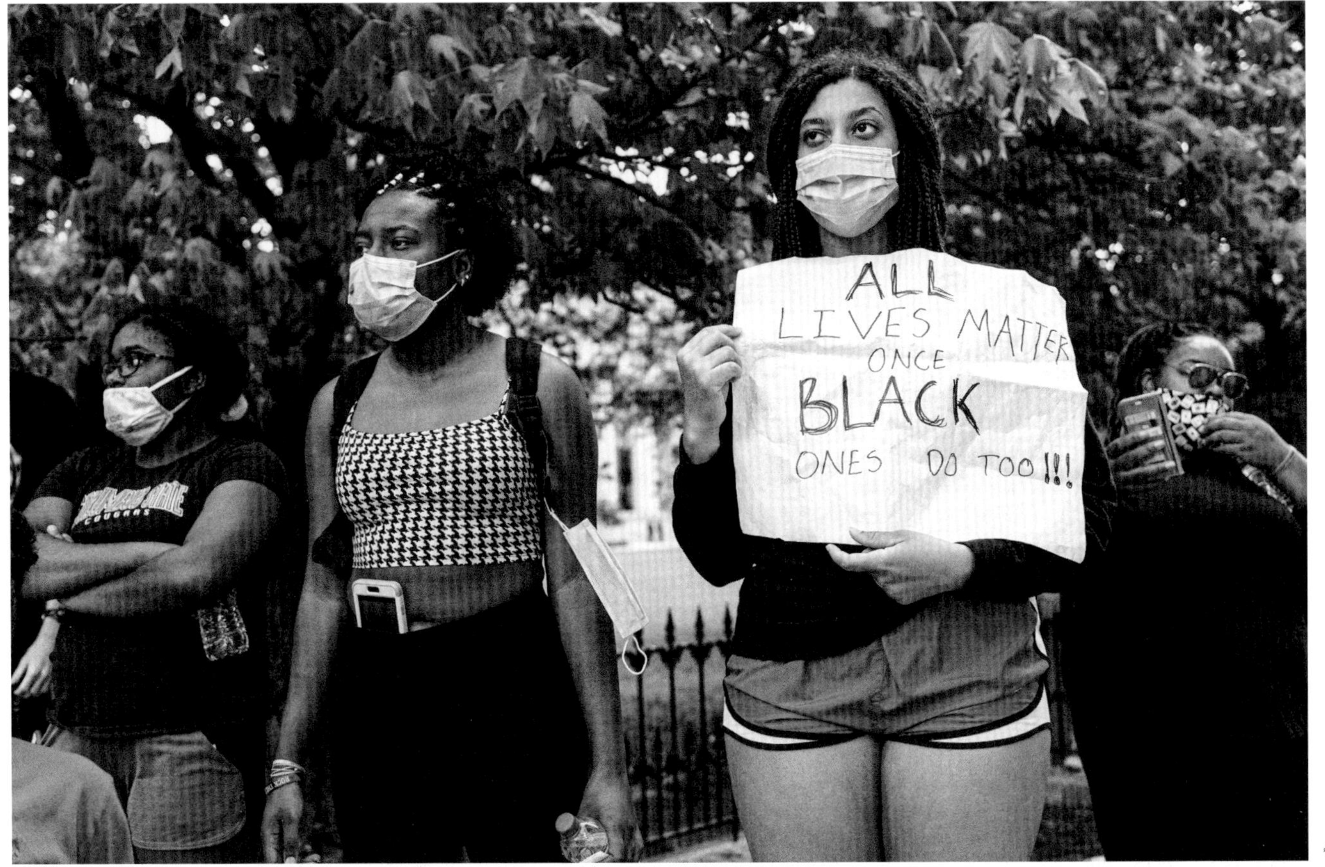
ALL
LIVES MATTER
ONCE
BLACK
ONES   DO TOO!!!

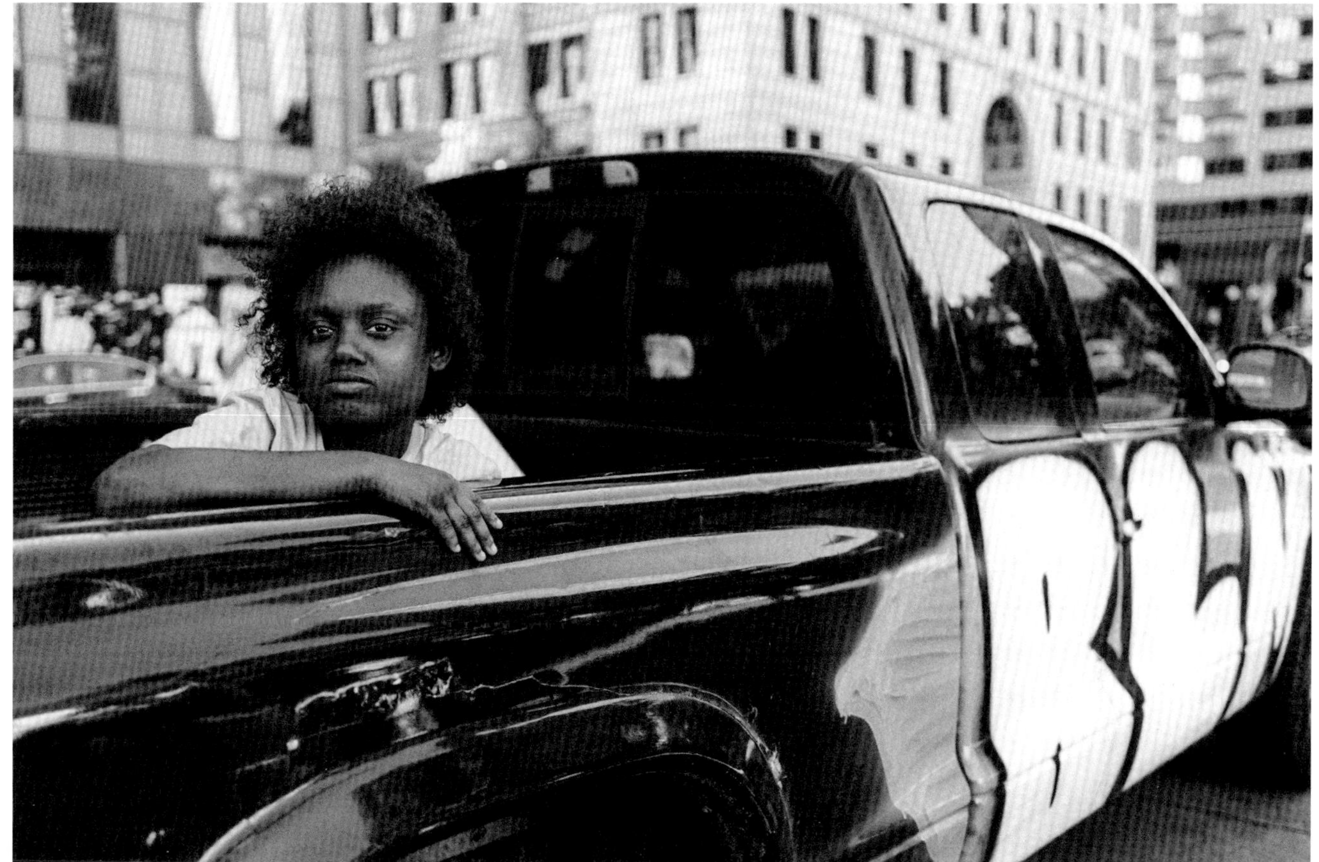
BLM

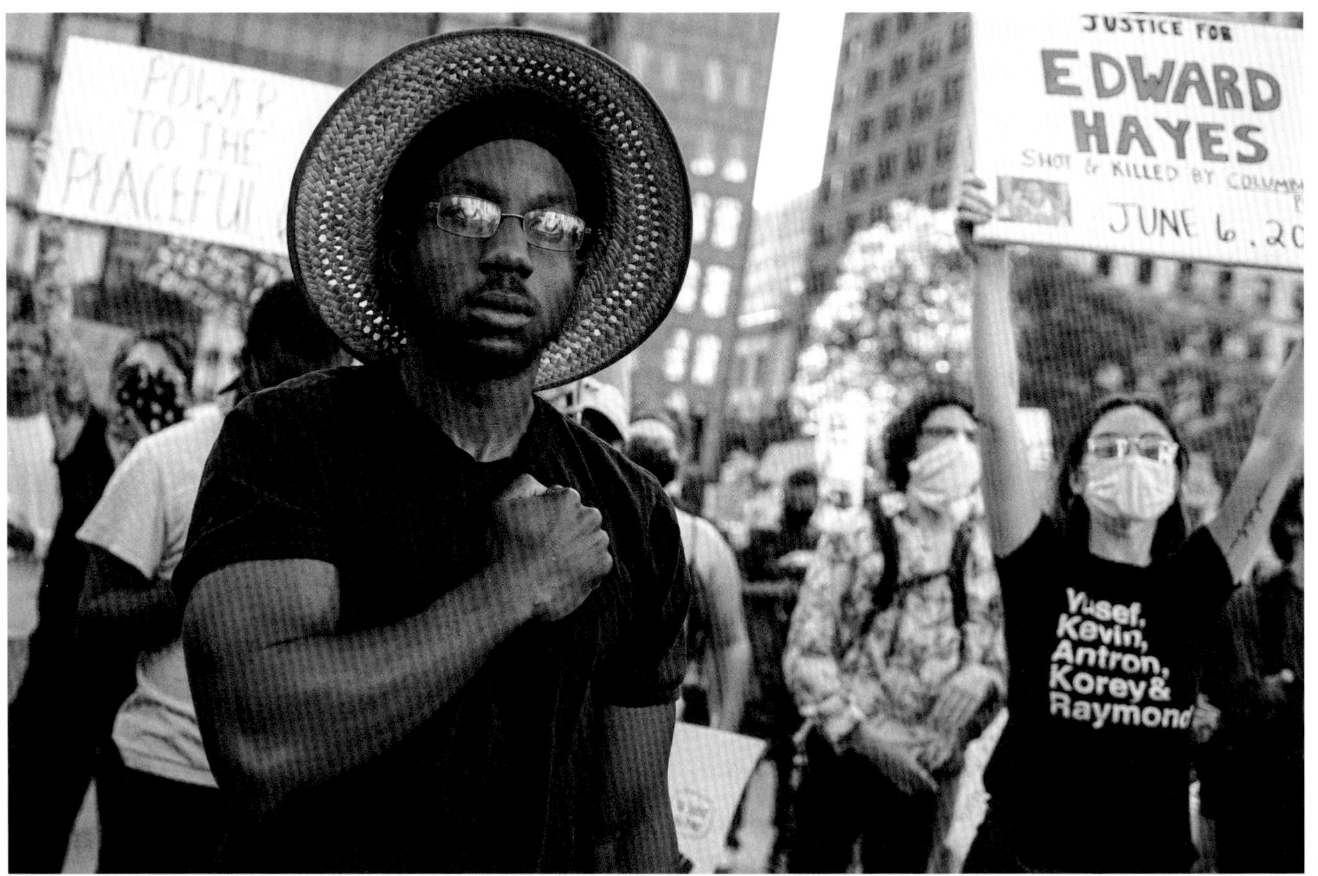
POWER
TO THE
PEACEFUL
JUSTICE FOR
EDWARD
HAYES
SHOT & KILLED BY COLUMB
JUNE 6, 20
Yusef,
Kevin,
Antron,
Korey &
Raymond

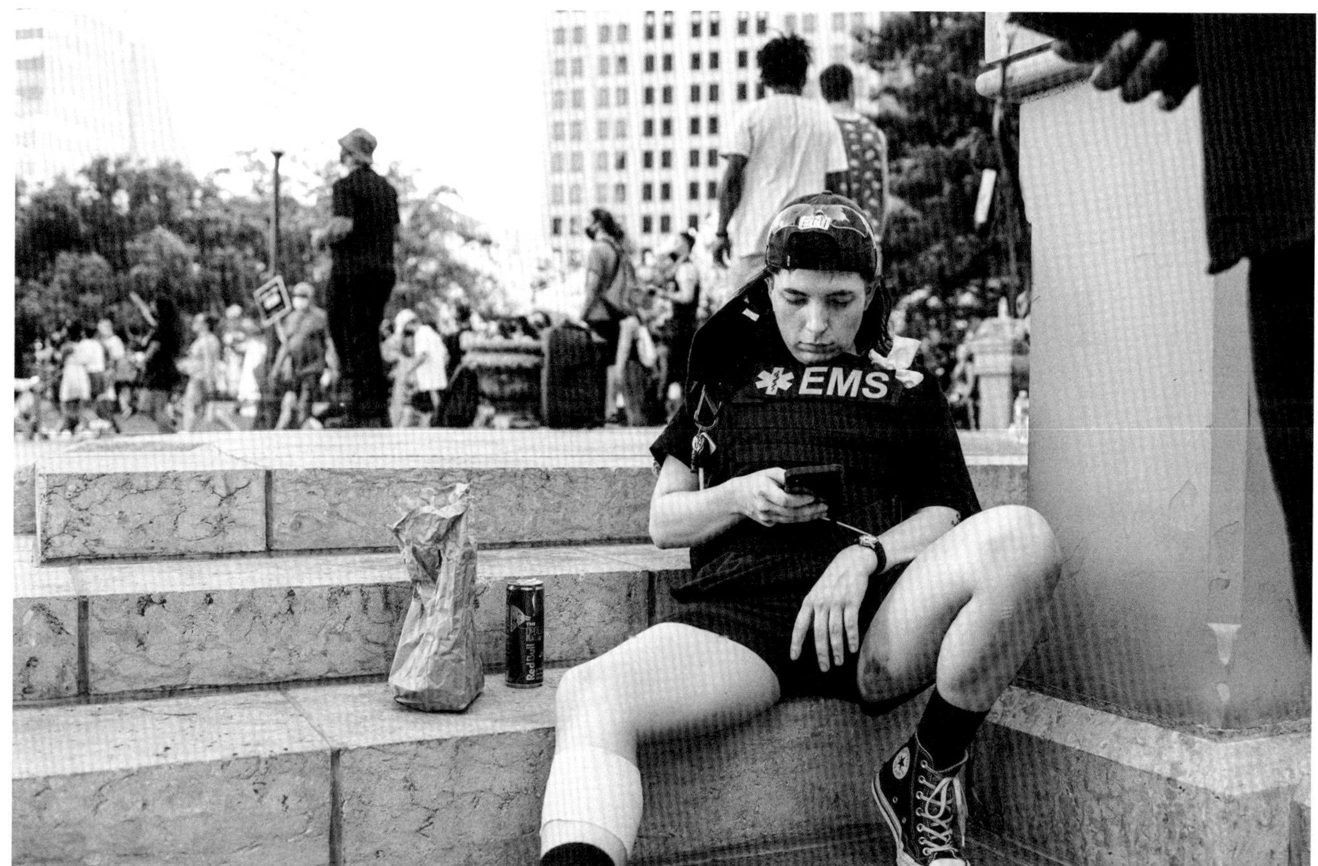

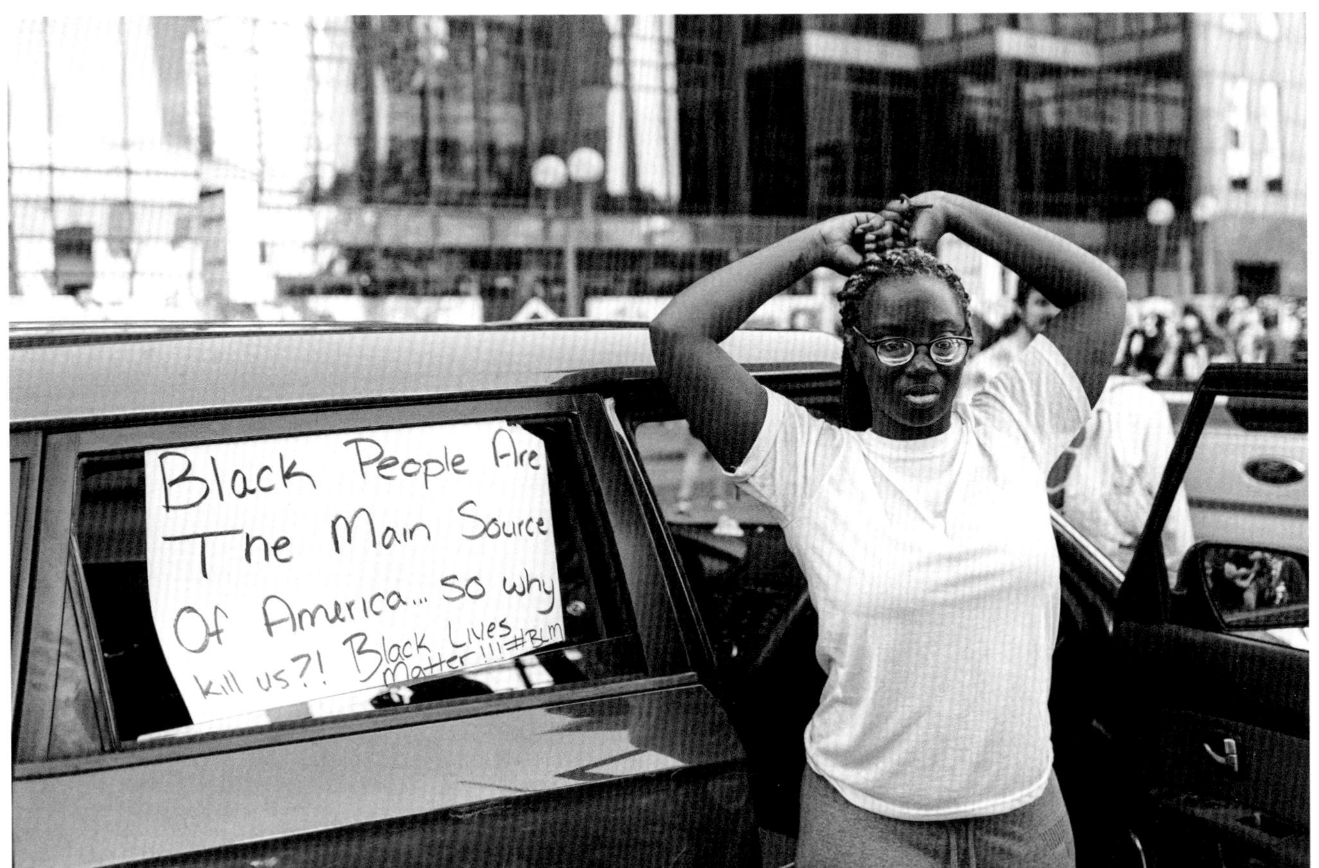

Black People Are The Main Source Of America... So Why kill us?! Black Lives Matter!!! #BLM

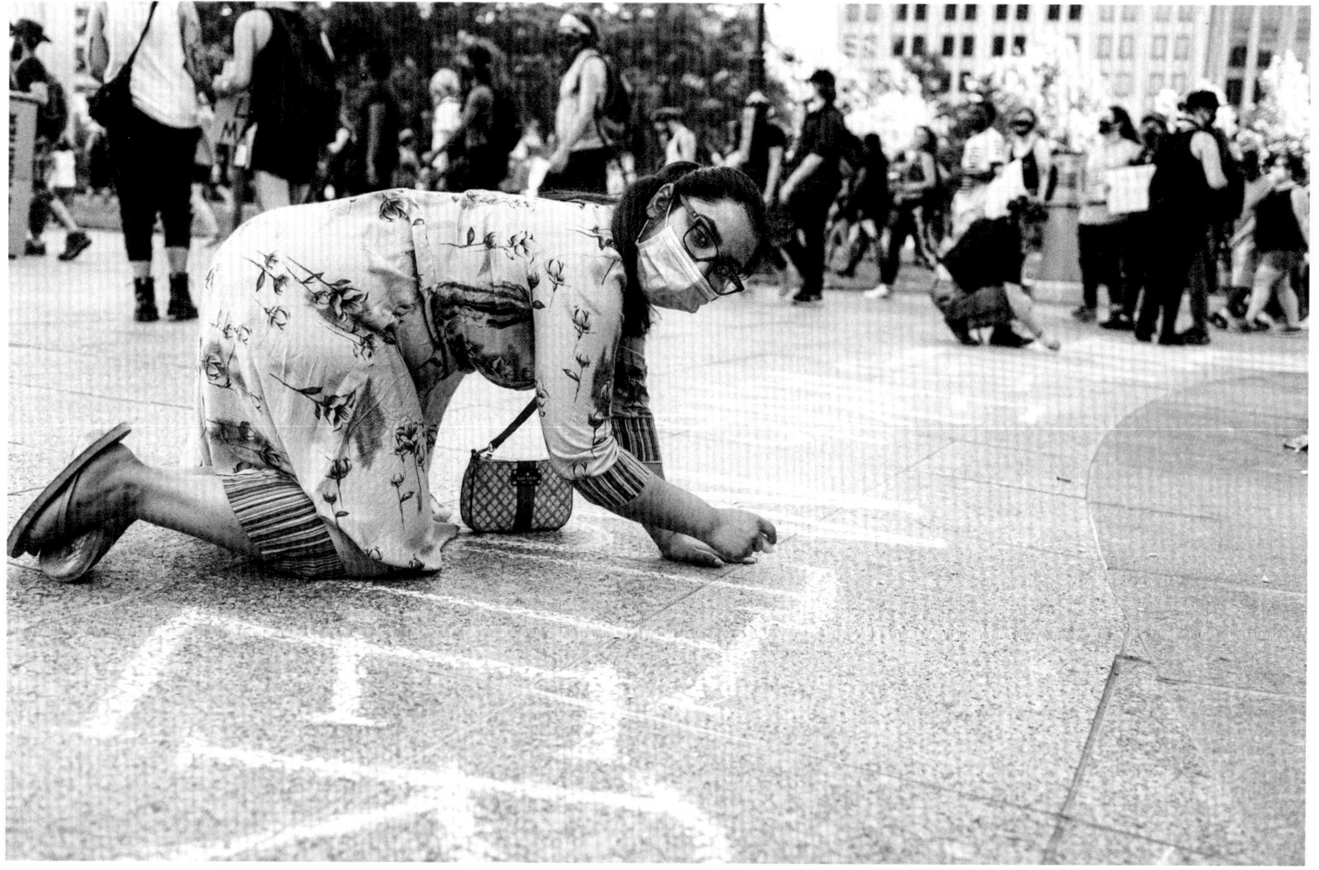

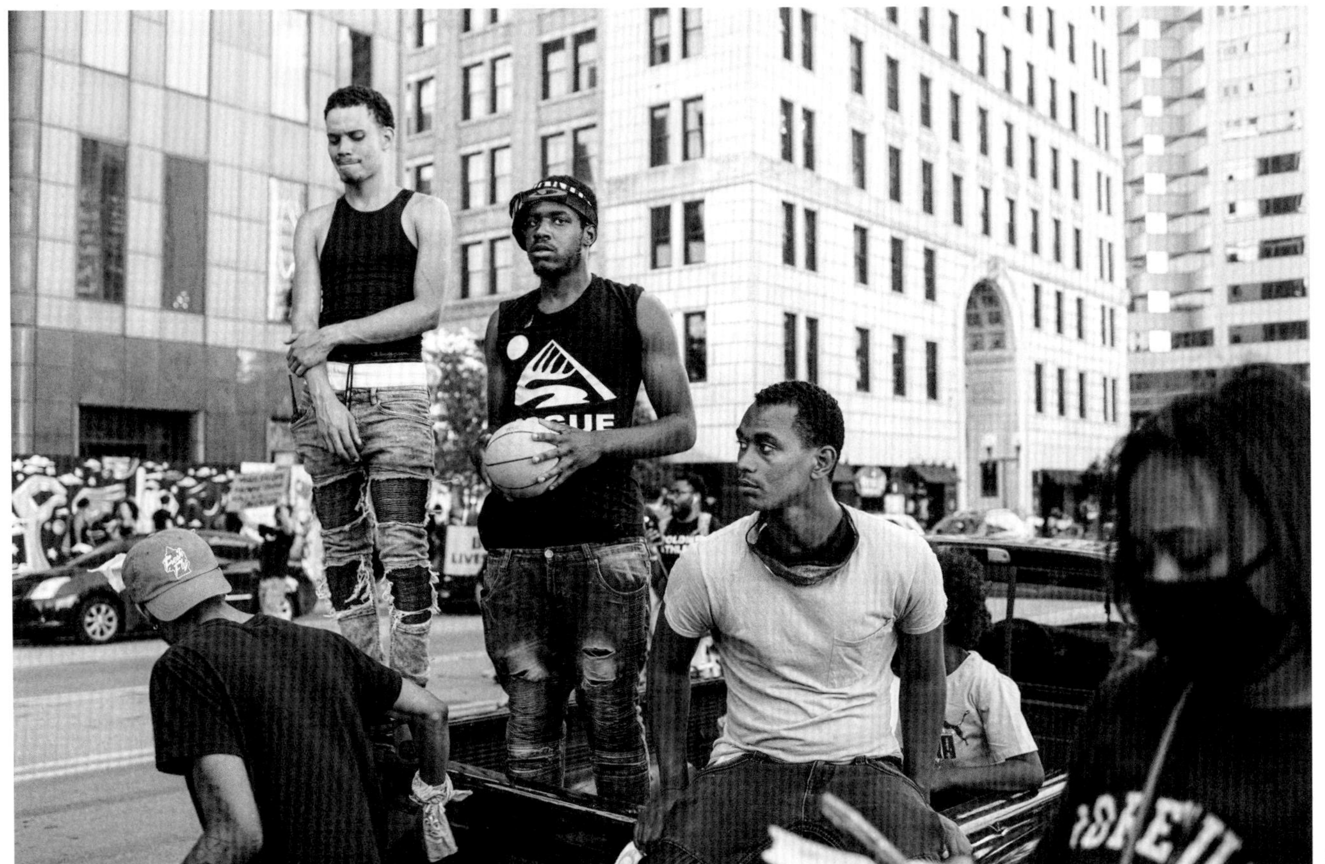

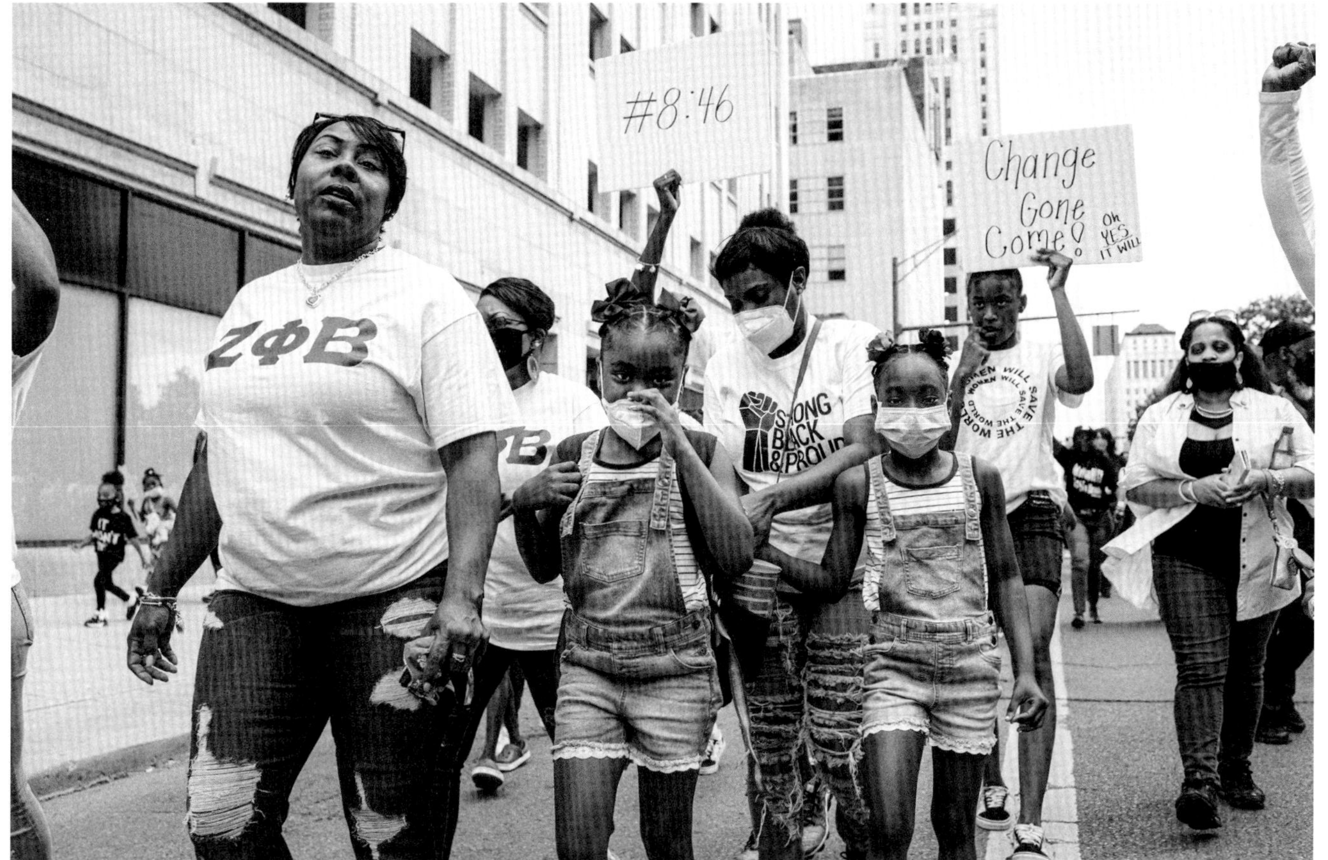
#8:46
Change Gone Come! Oh YES IT WILL
ZΦB
STRONG BLACK & PROUD
WOMEN WILL SAVE THE WORLD

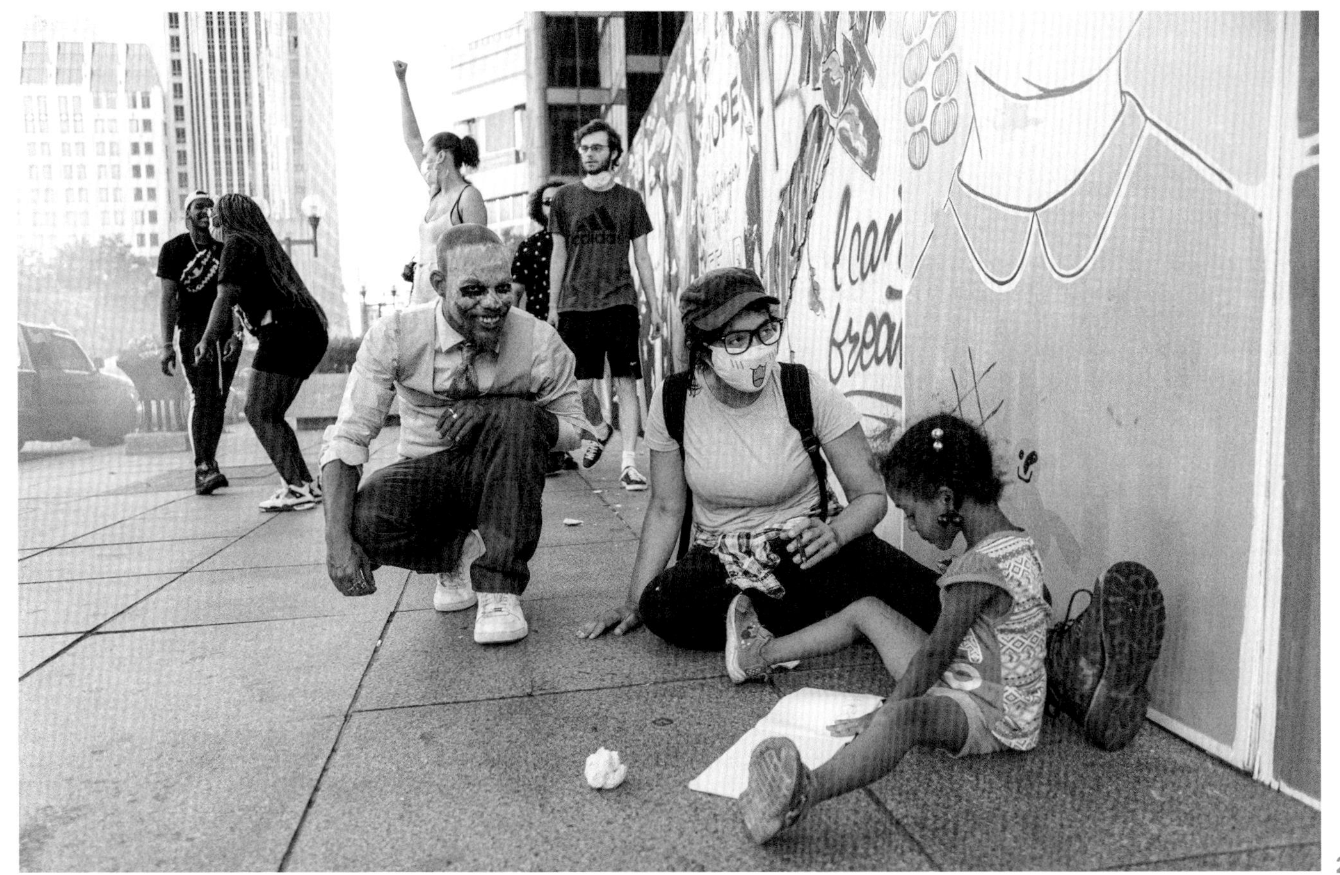

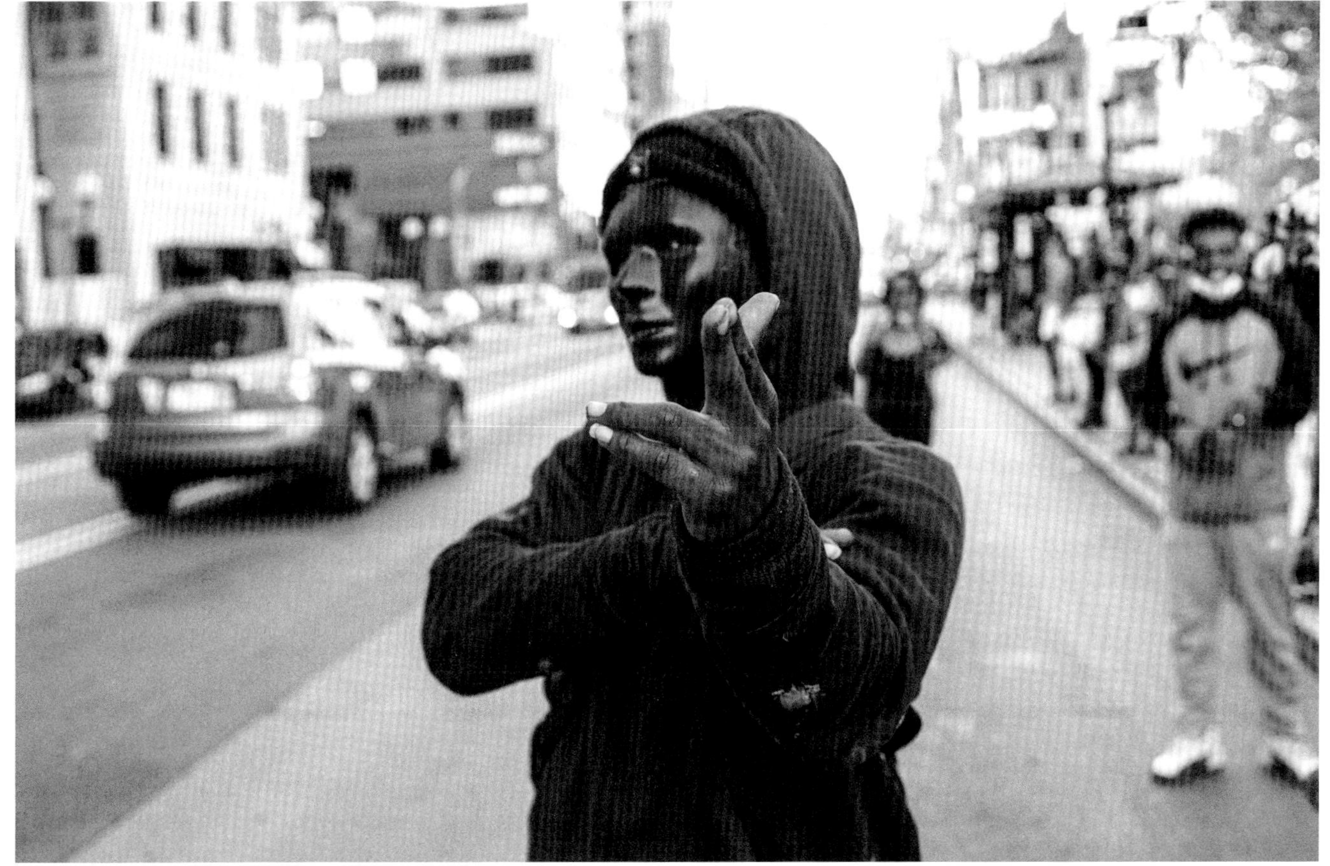

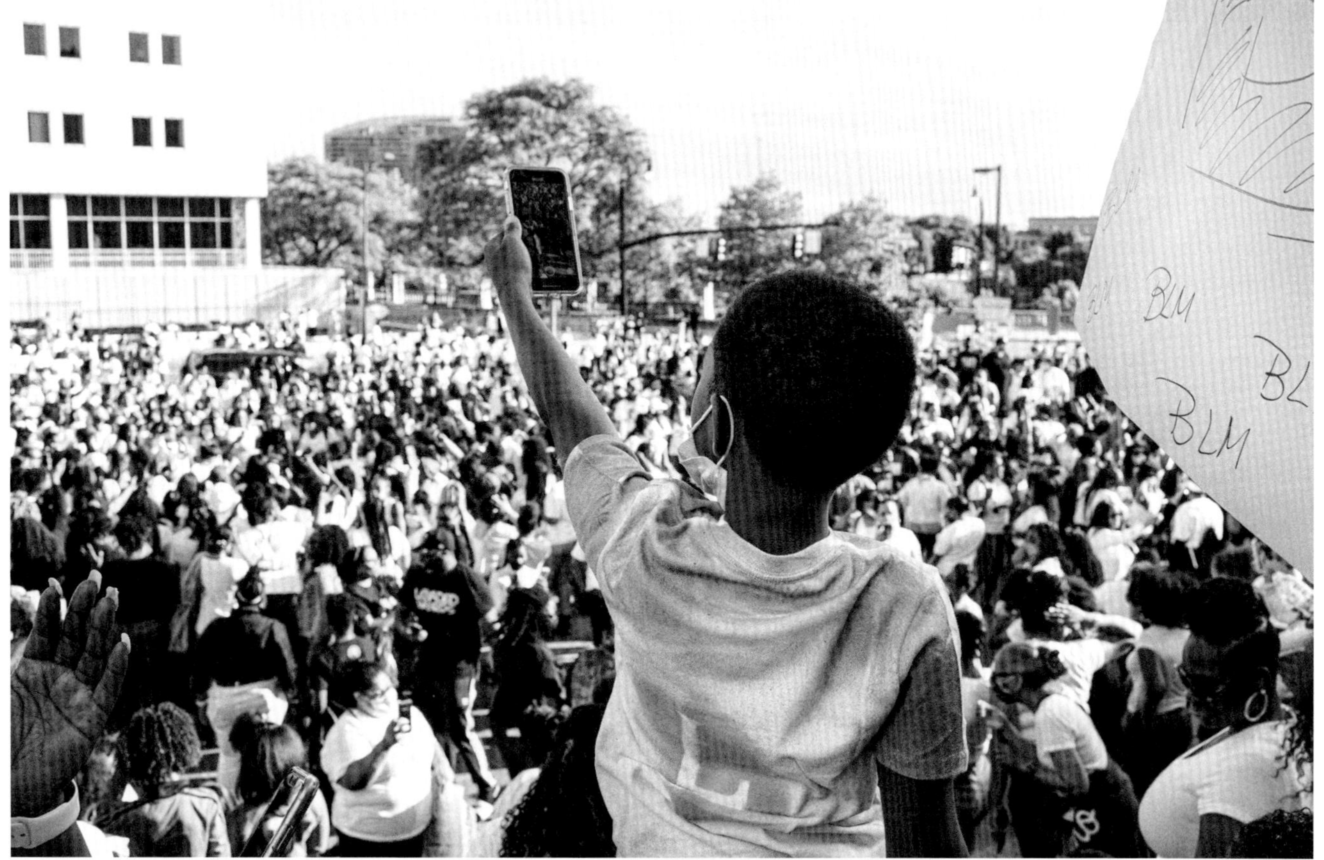
BLM
BLM
BLM
BL

Ohio Theatre
"THE TIME IS ALWAYS RIGHT TO DO WHAT IS RIGHT"
- MARTIN LUTHER KING JR.
CAPA WELCO
STATE THEATRE OF OHIO   TIONAL LANDMARK
EVEN THE   ST
NIGHT W
AND

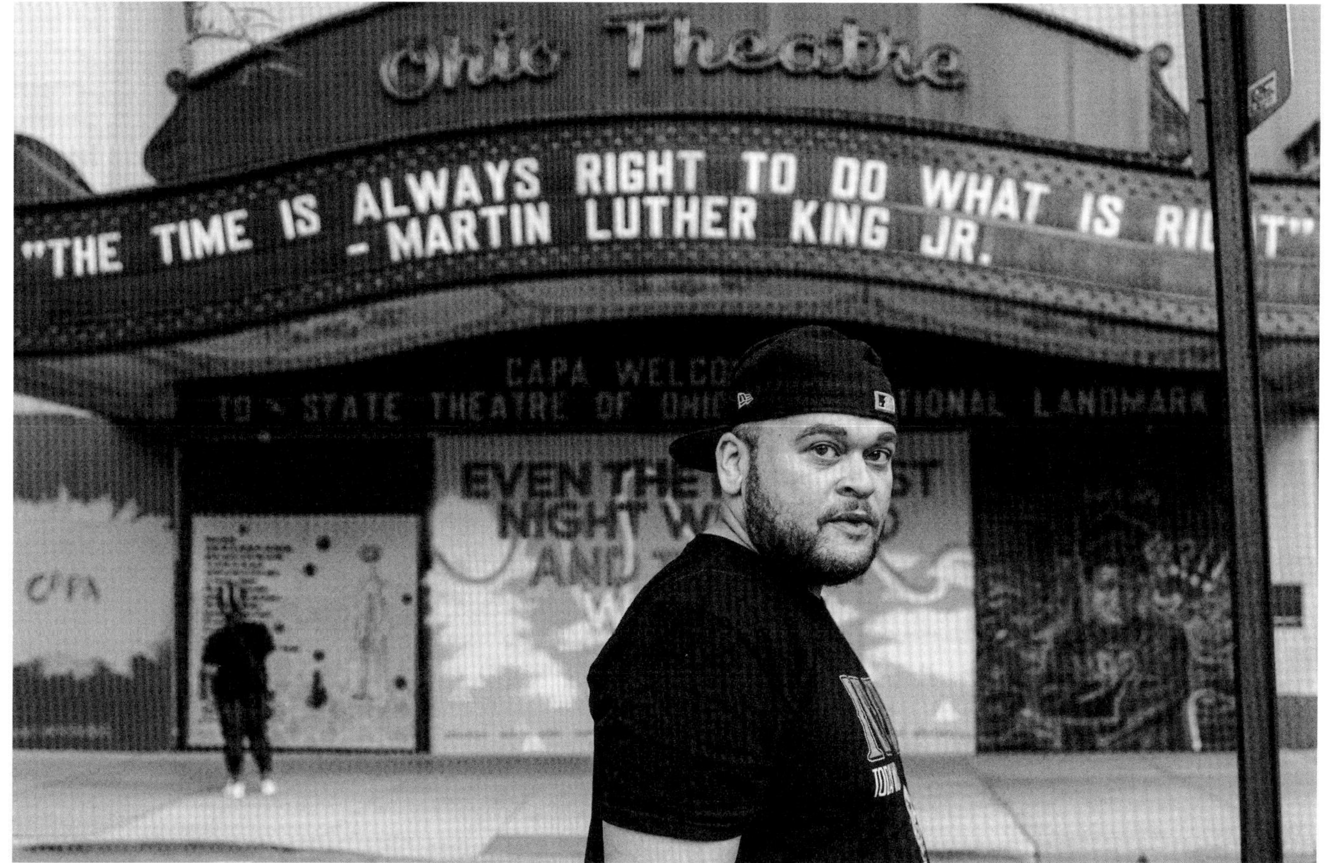

23

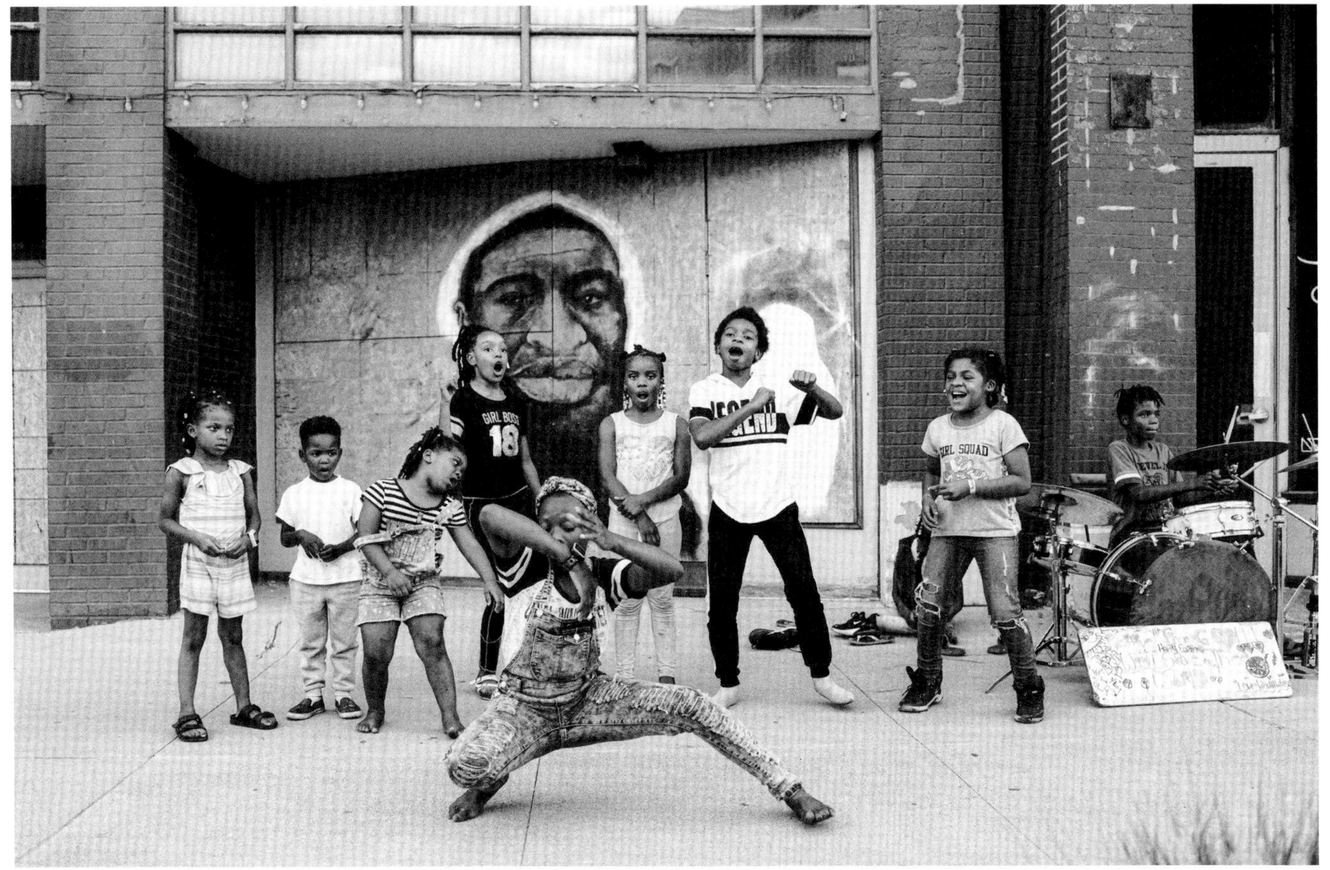
GIRL BOSS
18
LEGEND
GIRL SQUAD

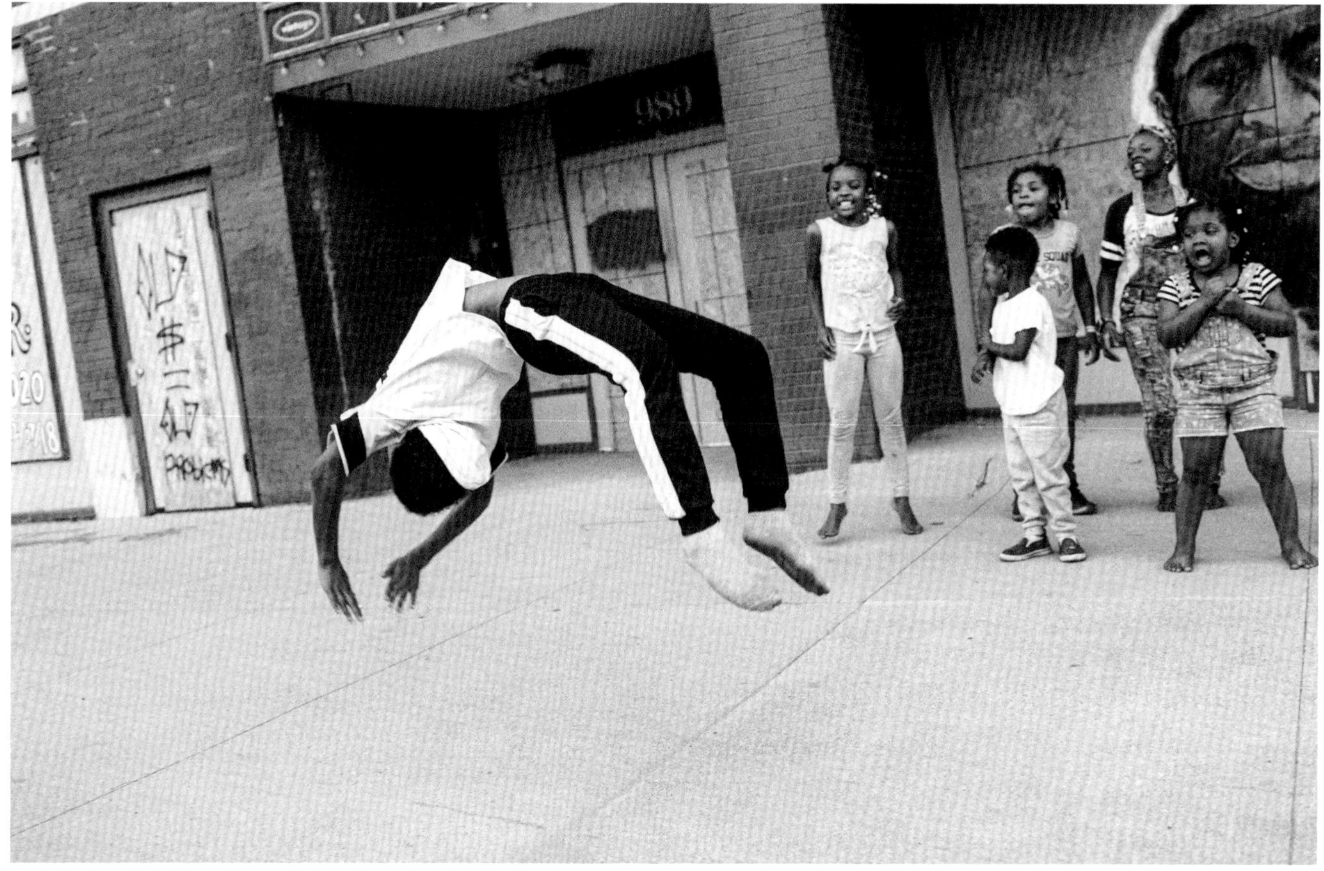

II.

Heedful Hold

An indefinite walk through a long
icy underpass, a bus

elapsing at a velocity that seems
to deform the flank's advertisement,

the large faces of the ad's actors
rendered ghostly and moaning.

—

Our work mutates; our children become
disallowed from group play. Our children

schooled via numbing screens. Our children more
quickly adopt the bafflement of adults.

—

Weeping alone, watching a wake
livestreamed on a funeral home's media page;

the departed—cropped wrongly
by the mounted smartphone—

is someone whose staunch voice and gentle touch
fed many of us, we who shared

their sector of a land wrought
with laws and apathy that hunt us.

—

Where aggressors destroy
for fleeting dollars, when history's residues,

refurbished injustice, and a virus
collaborate to crush the moss of our sleep,

we hold our babies heedfully,
reconfirming we're the beautiful kin

of dignity's many mothers.

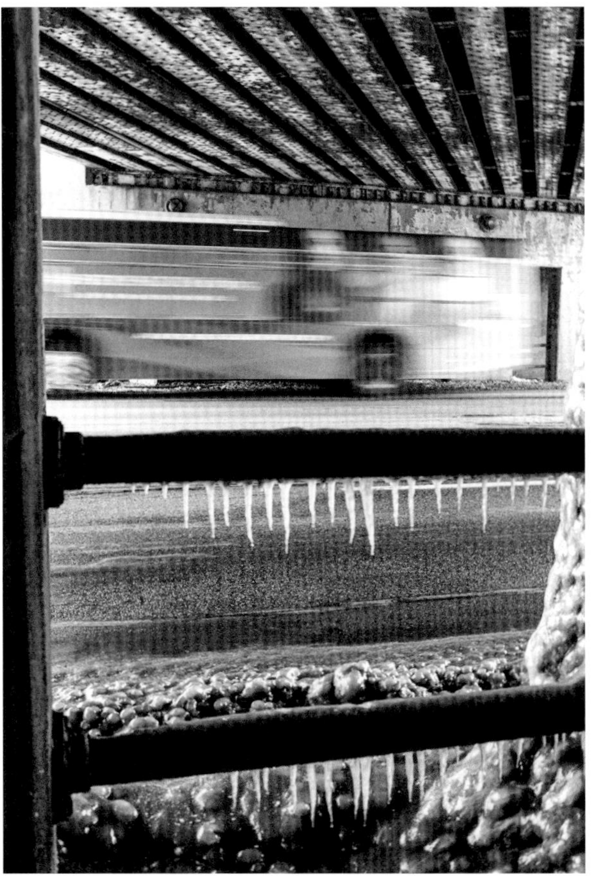

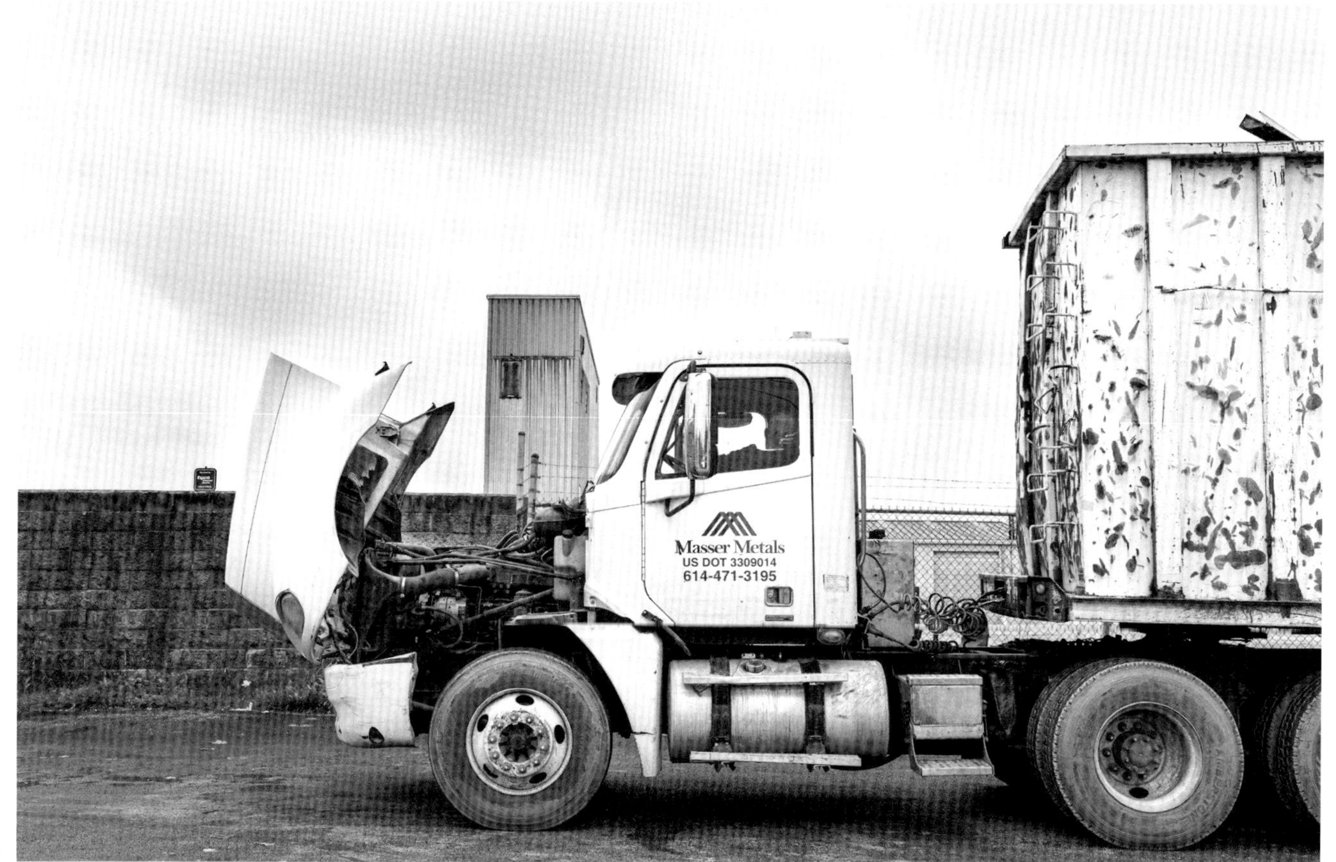

Masser Metals
US DOT 3309014
614-471-3195

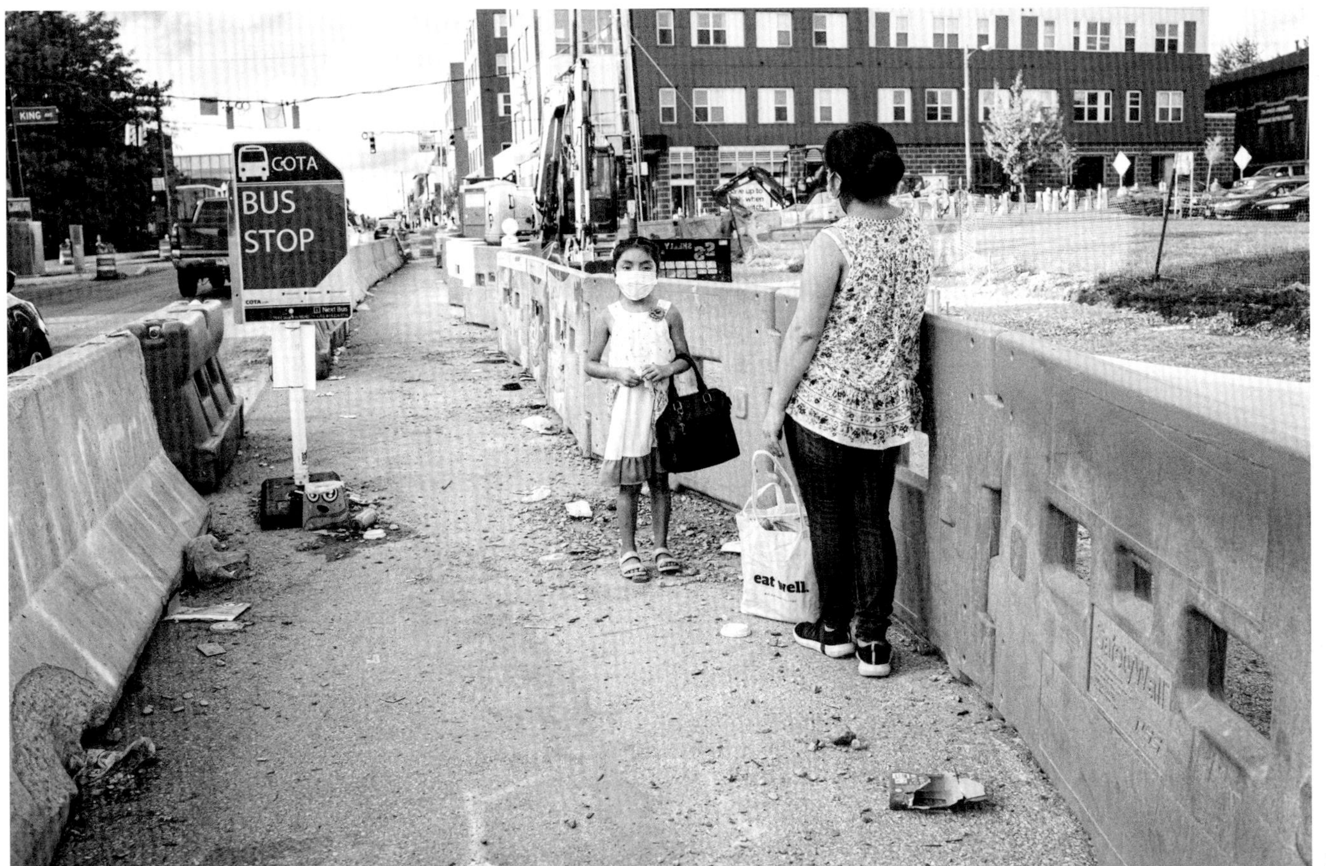
KING AVE
COTA
BUS
STOP
COTA.com
Next Bus
eat well.

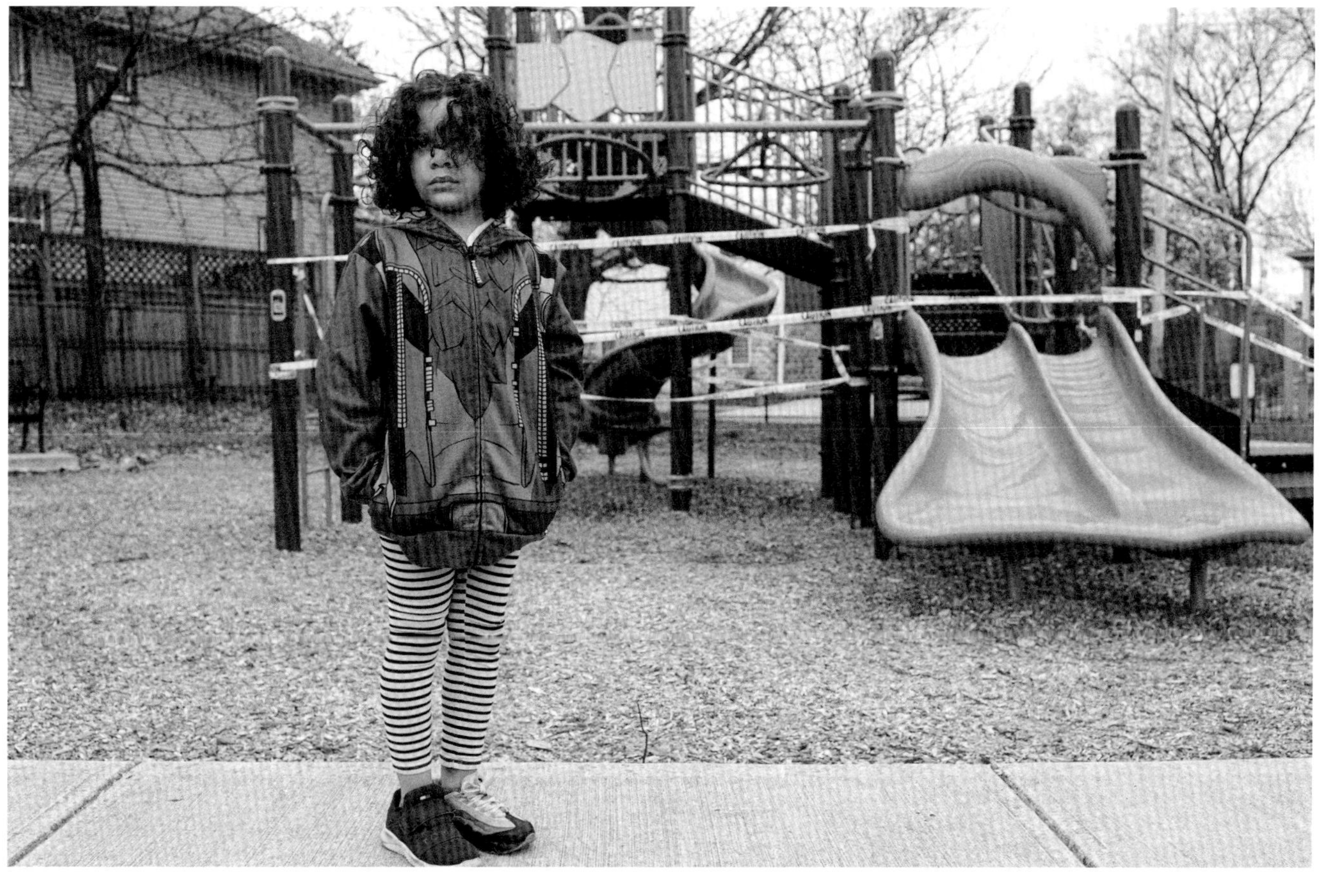

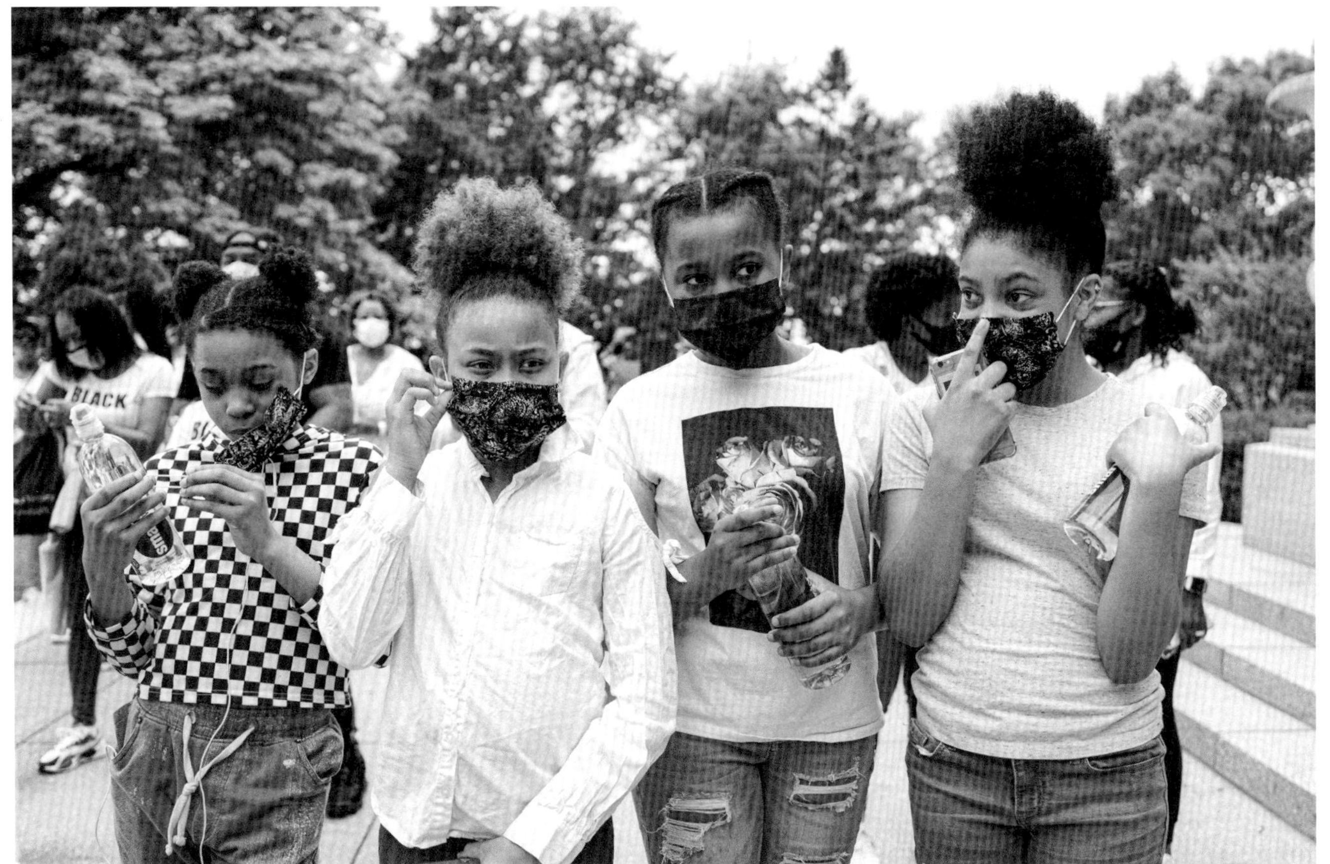

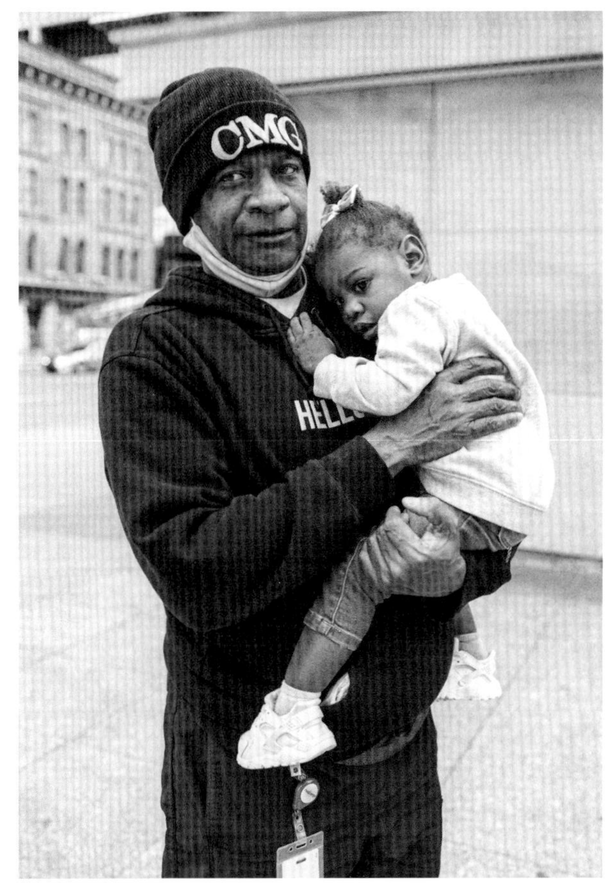

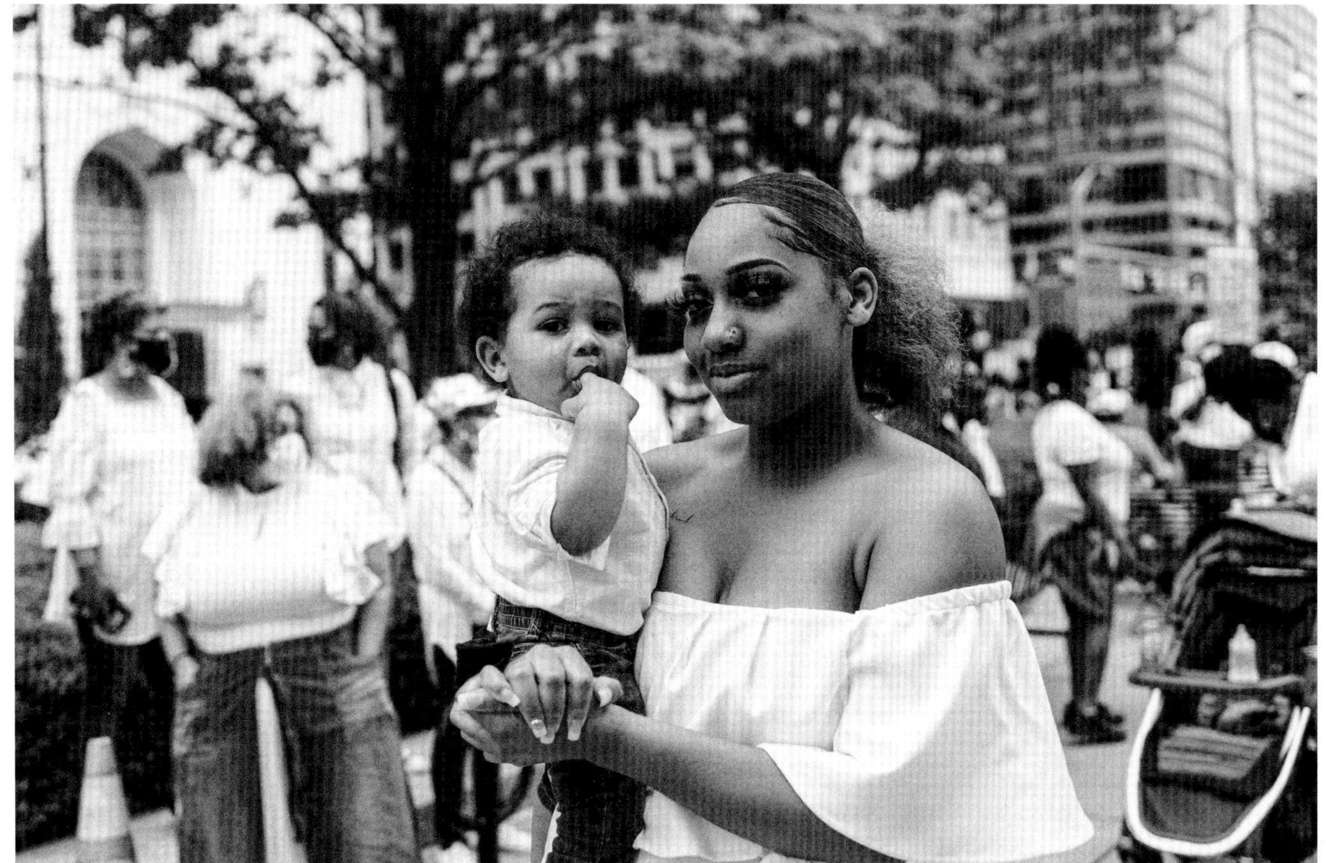

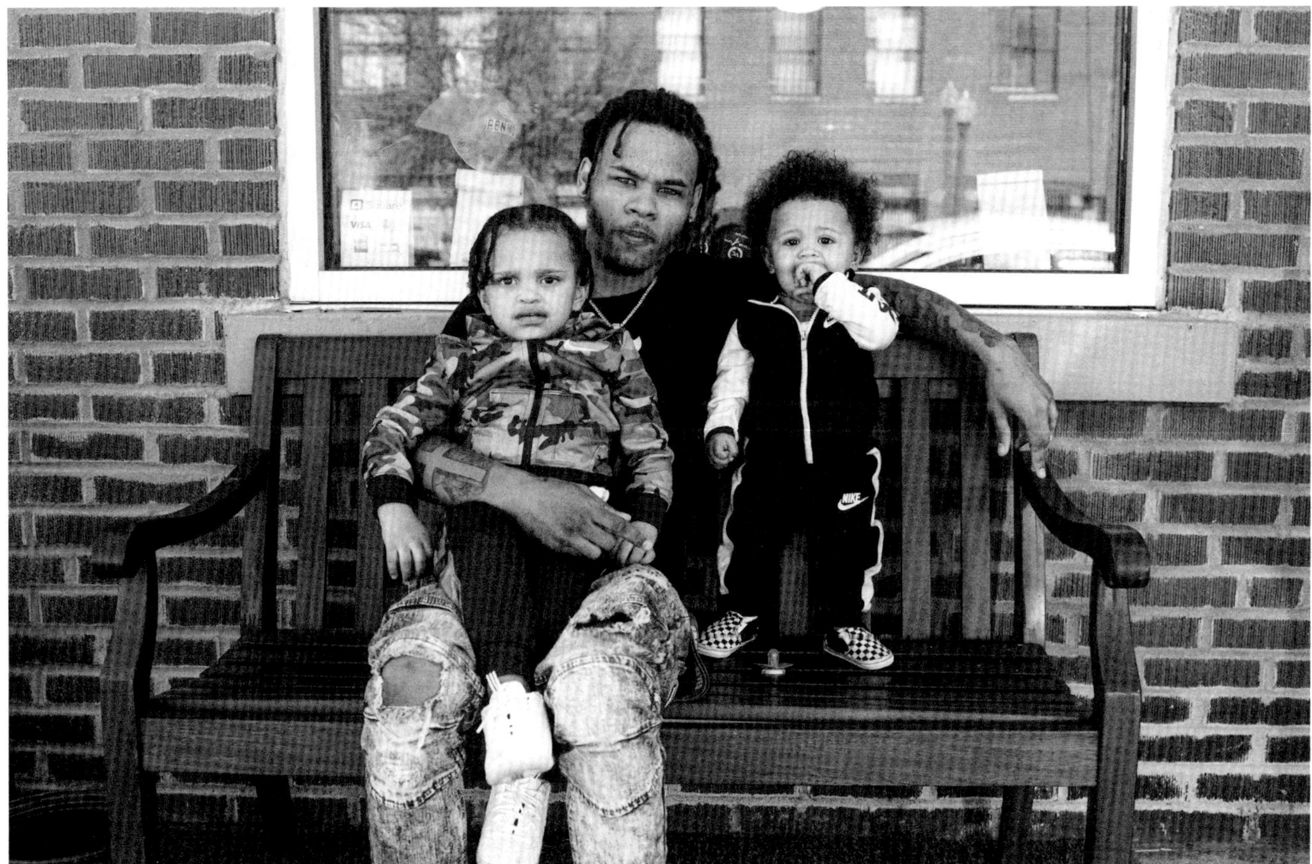

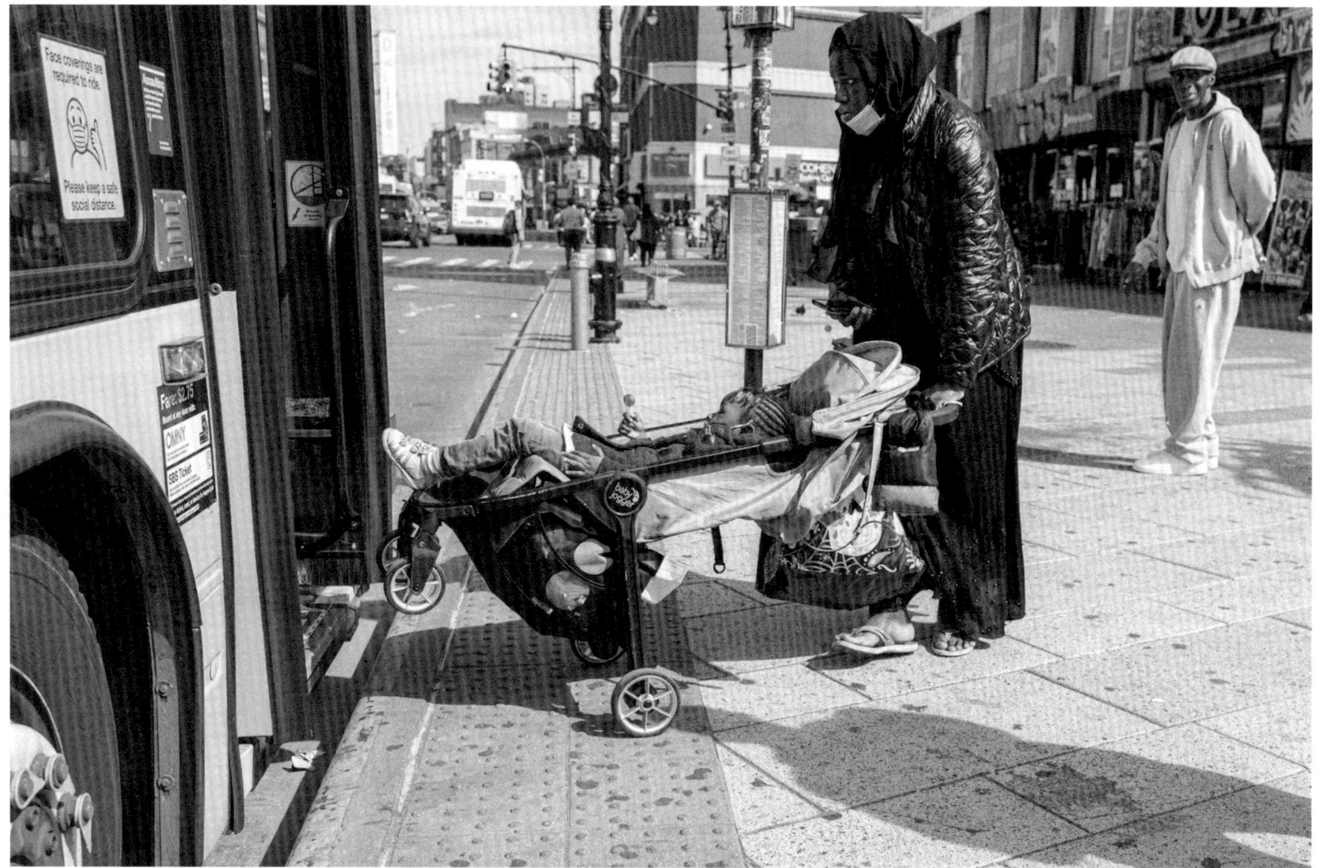

Face coverings are
required to ride.
Please keep a safe
social distance.
Fare: $2.75
OMNY
SBS Ticket
baby jogger

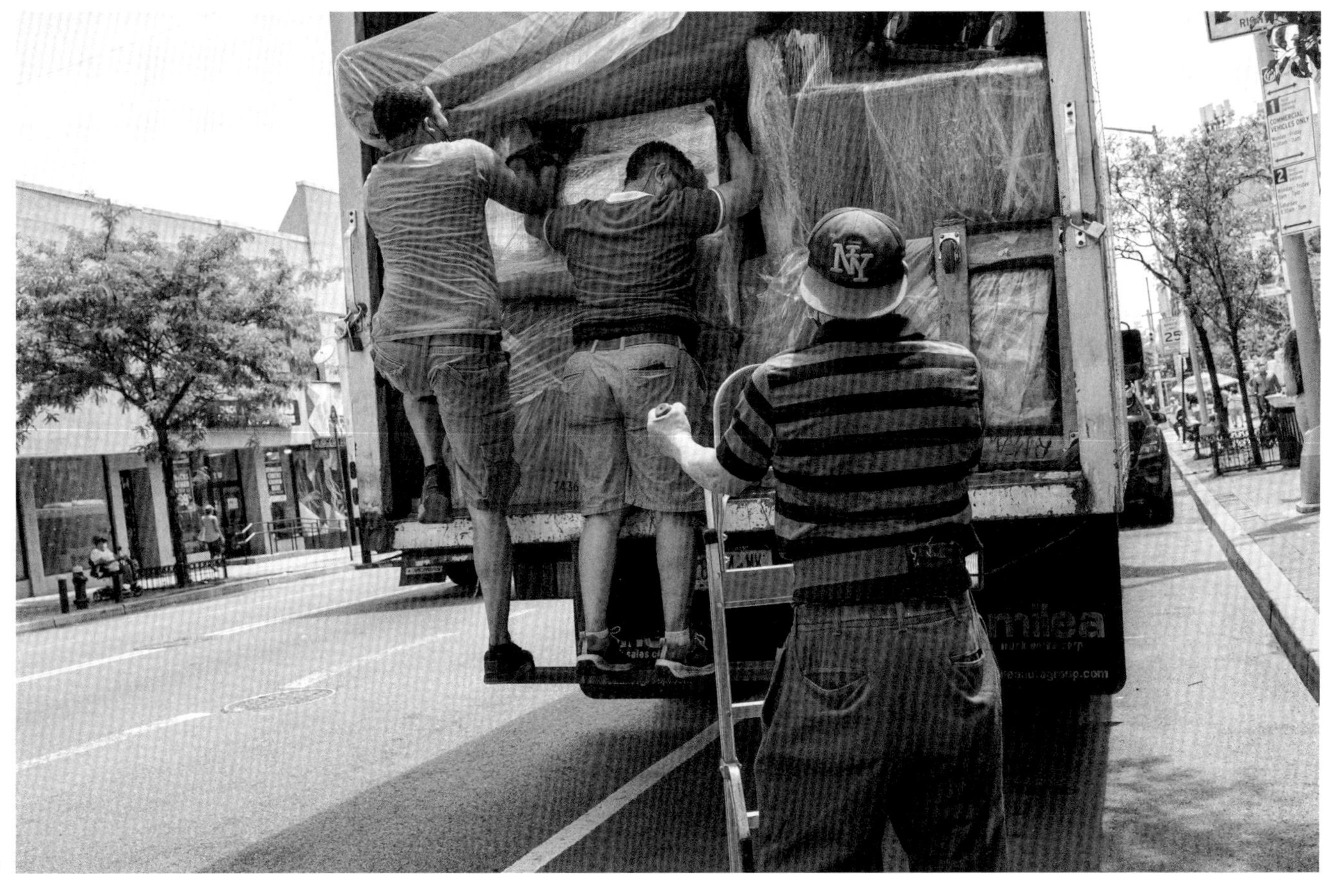

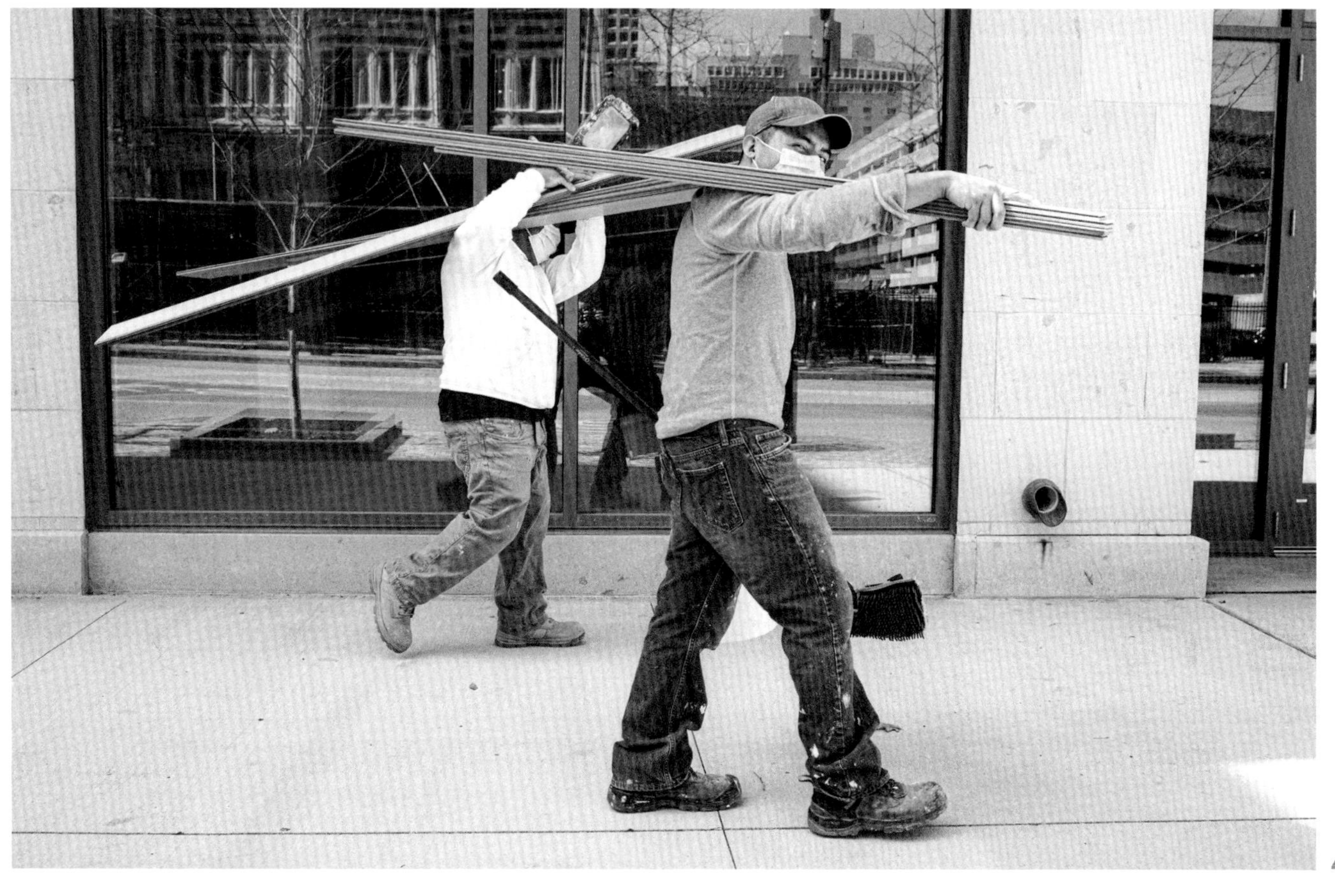

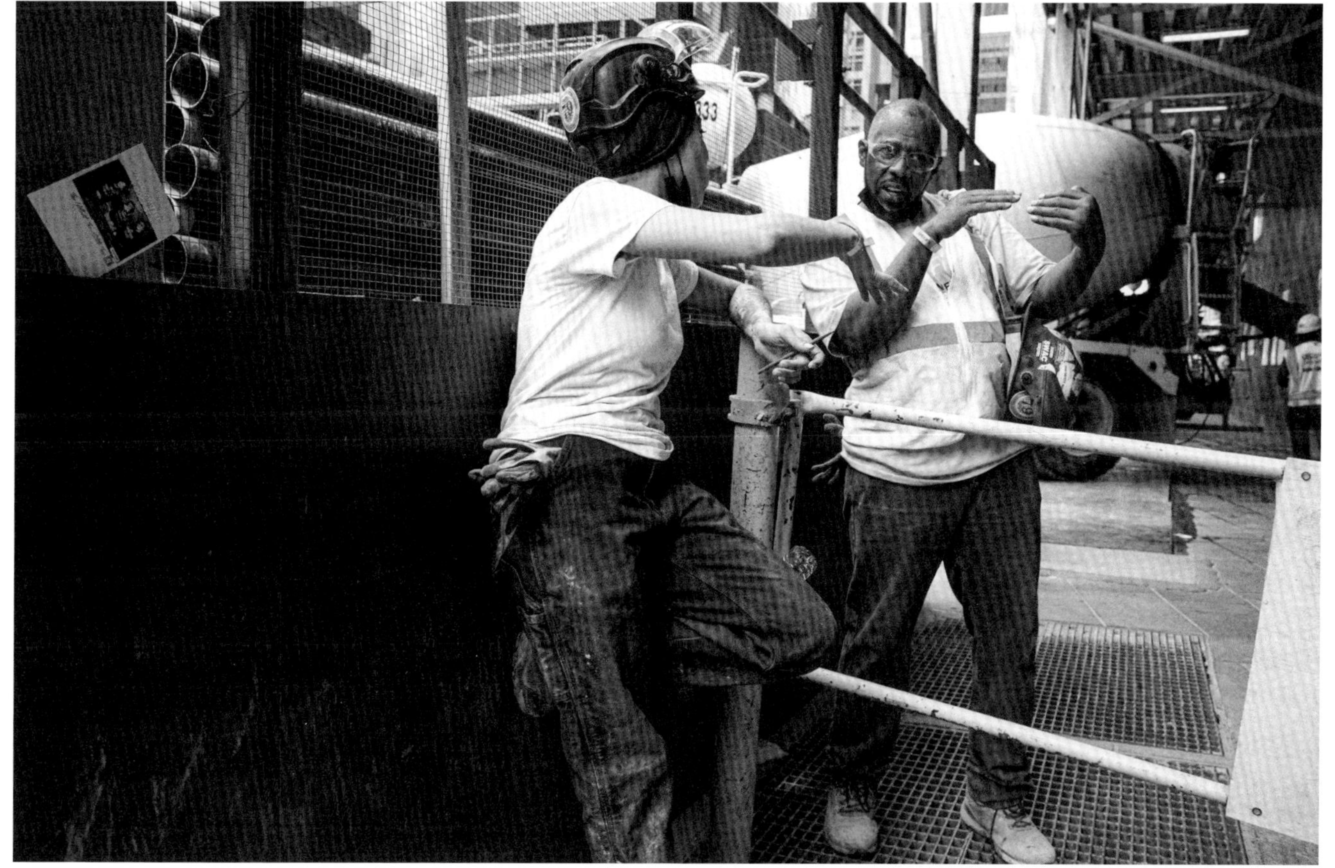

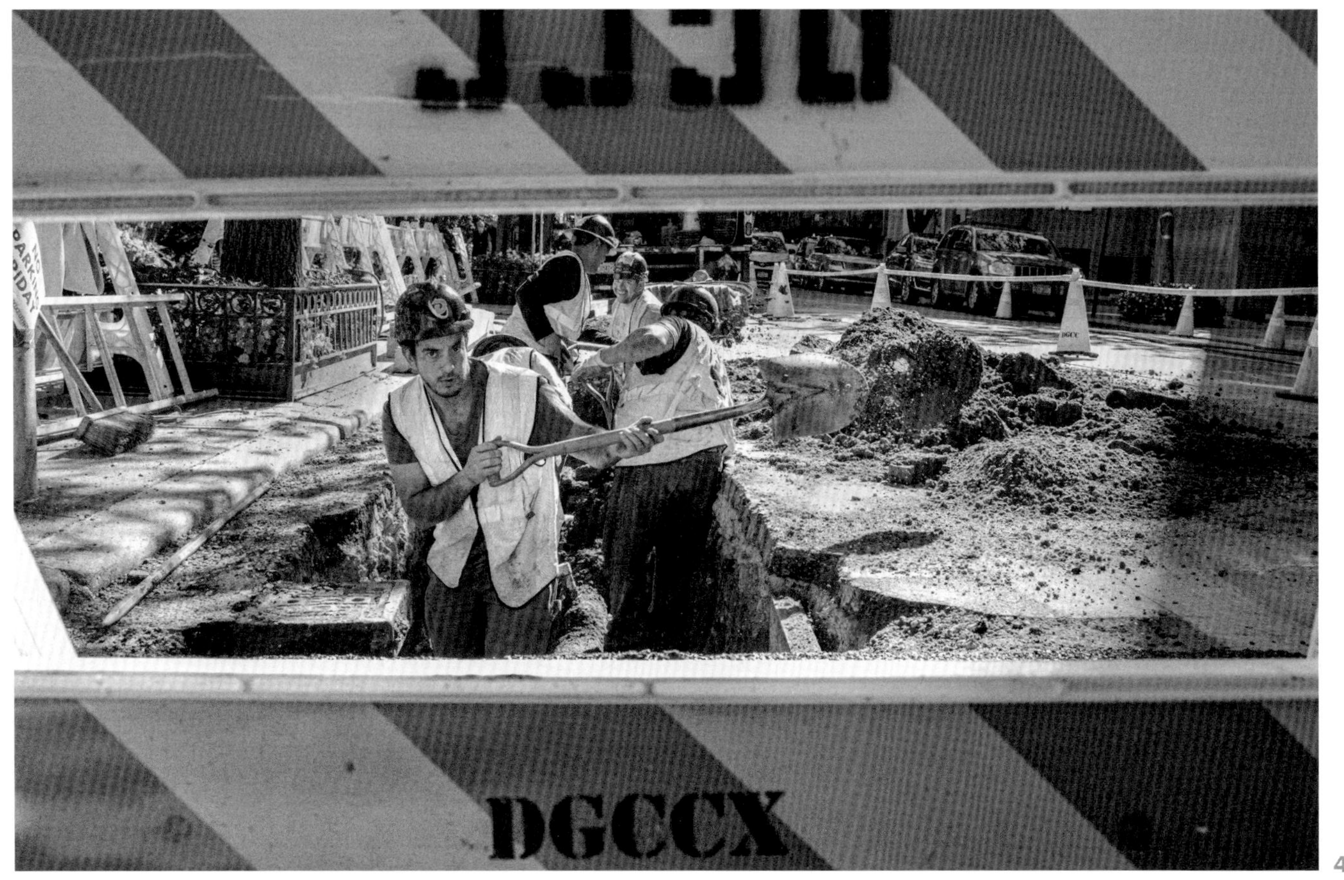
NO
PARKING
RIDAY
DGCCX

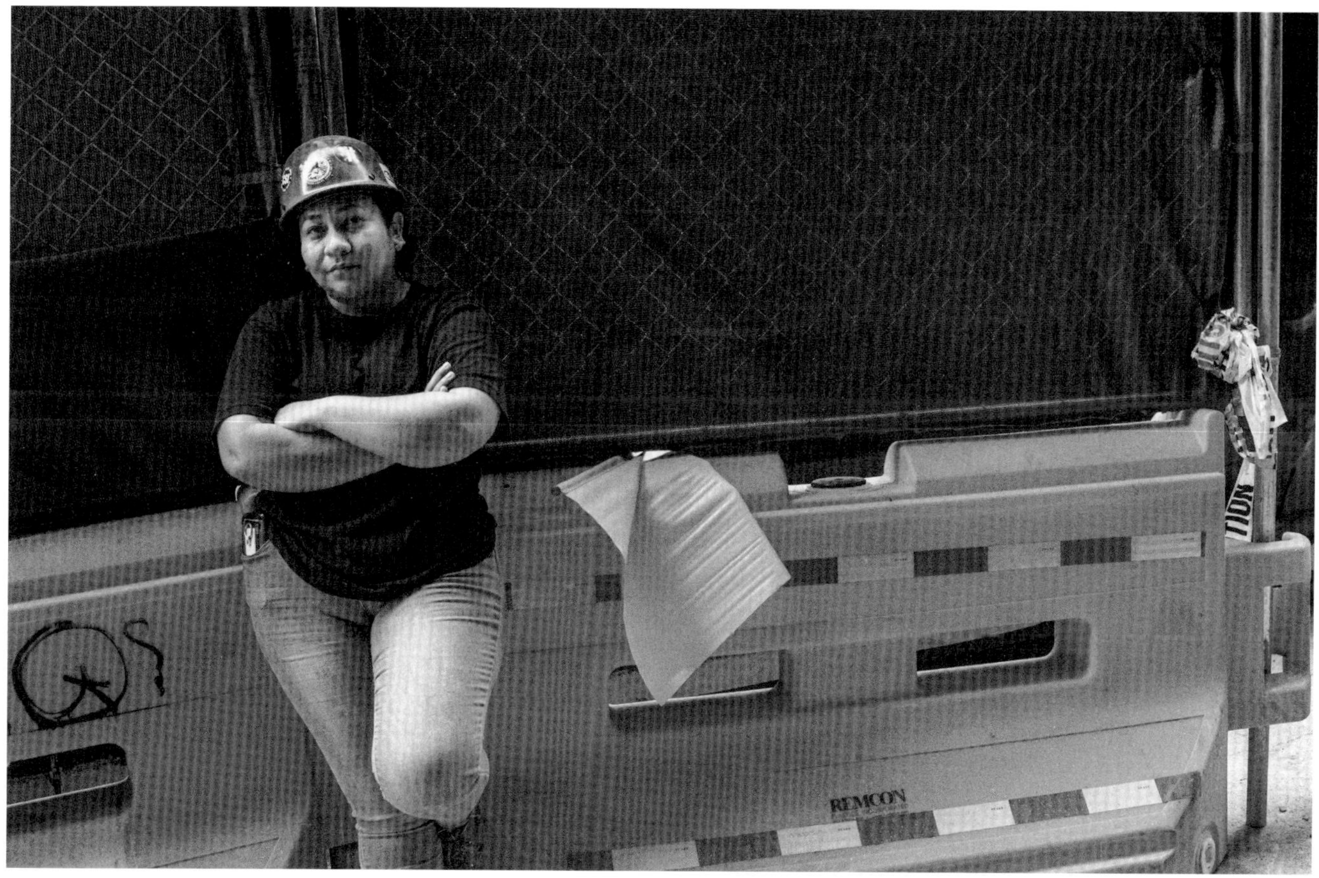

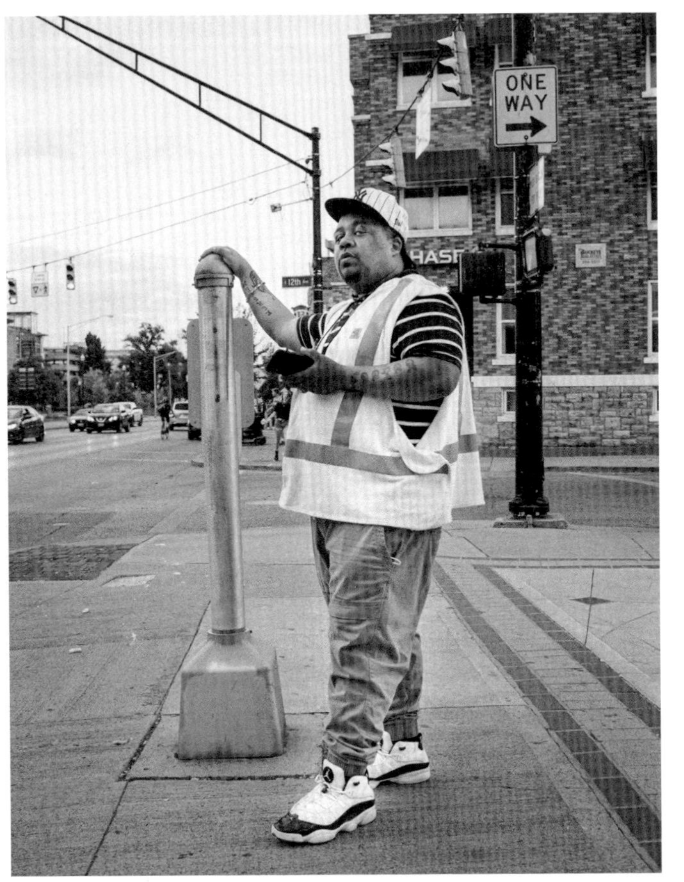
ONE
WAY

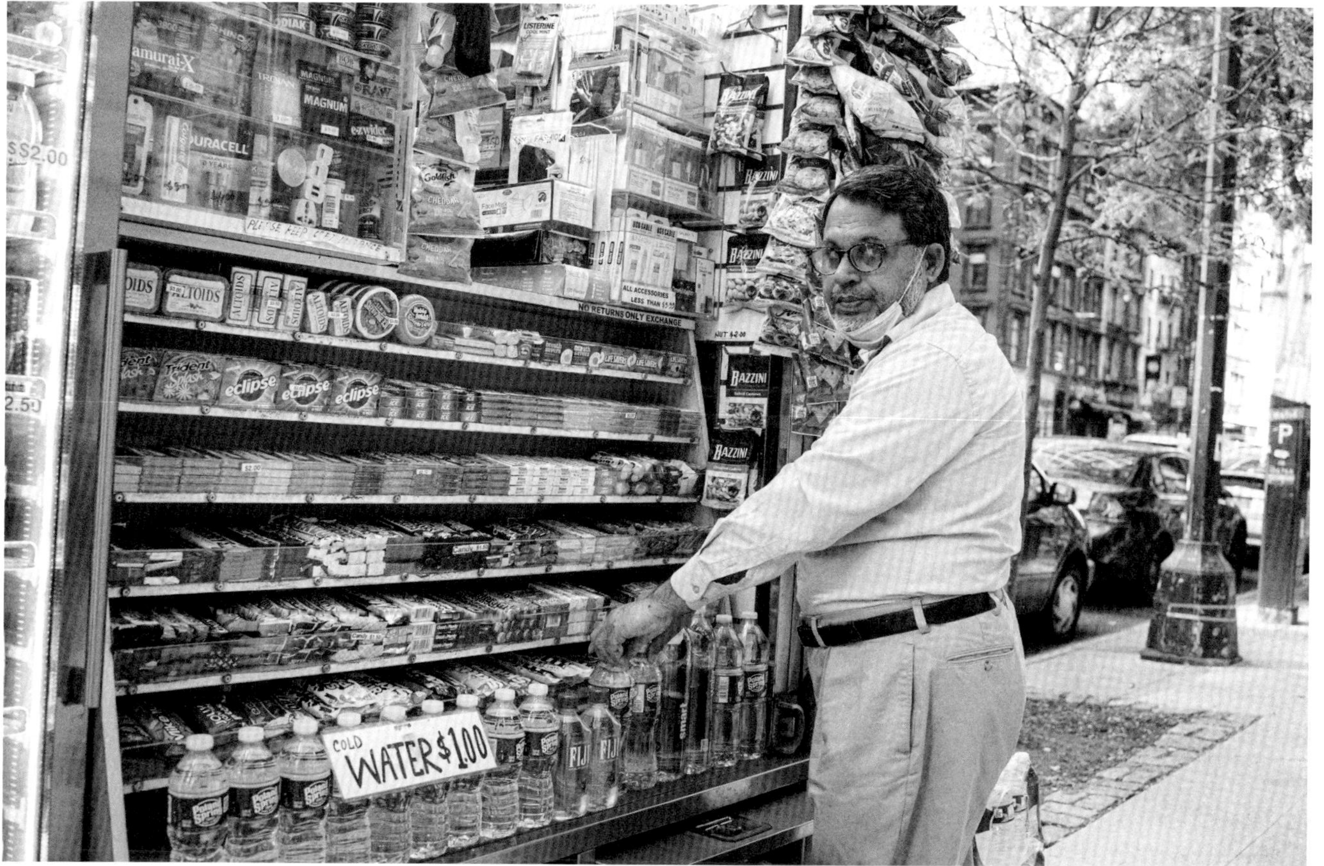
COLD WATER $1.00
NO RETURNS ONLY EXCHANGE
ALL ACCESSORIES LESS THAN $5.00
PLEASE KEEP 6FT DISTANCE
BAZZINI
DURACELL
MAGNUM
Samurai-X
LISTERINE
ALTOIDS
eclipse
Trident
$2.00
$2.50

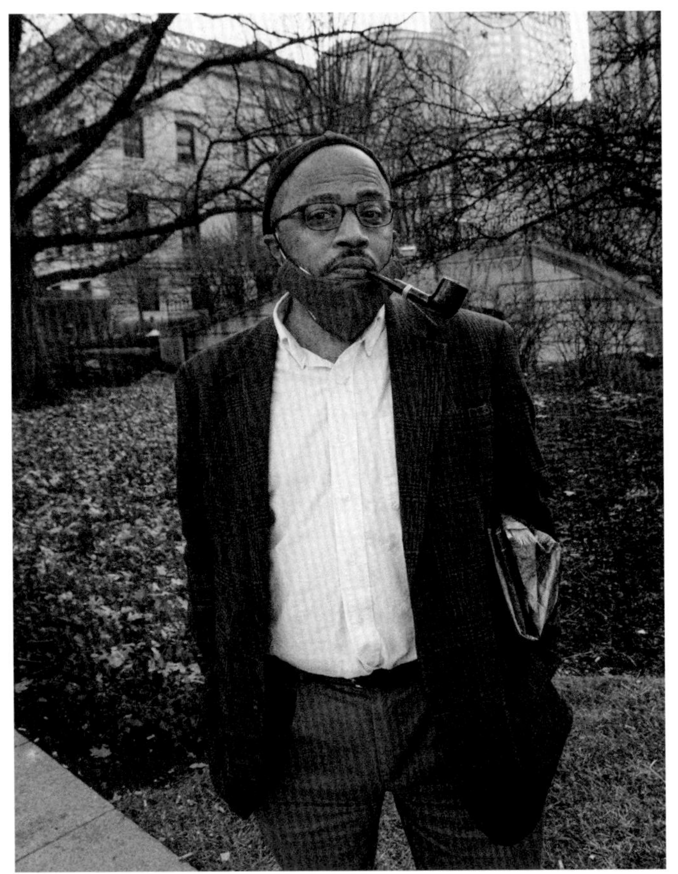

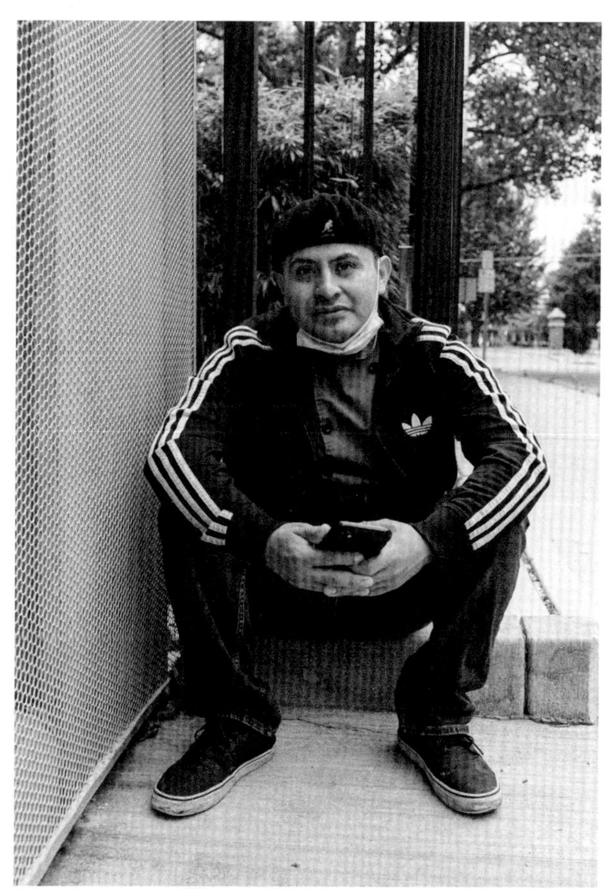

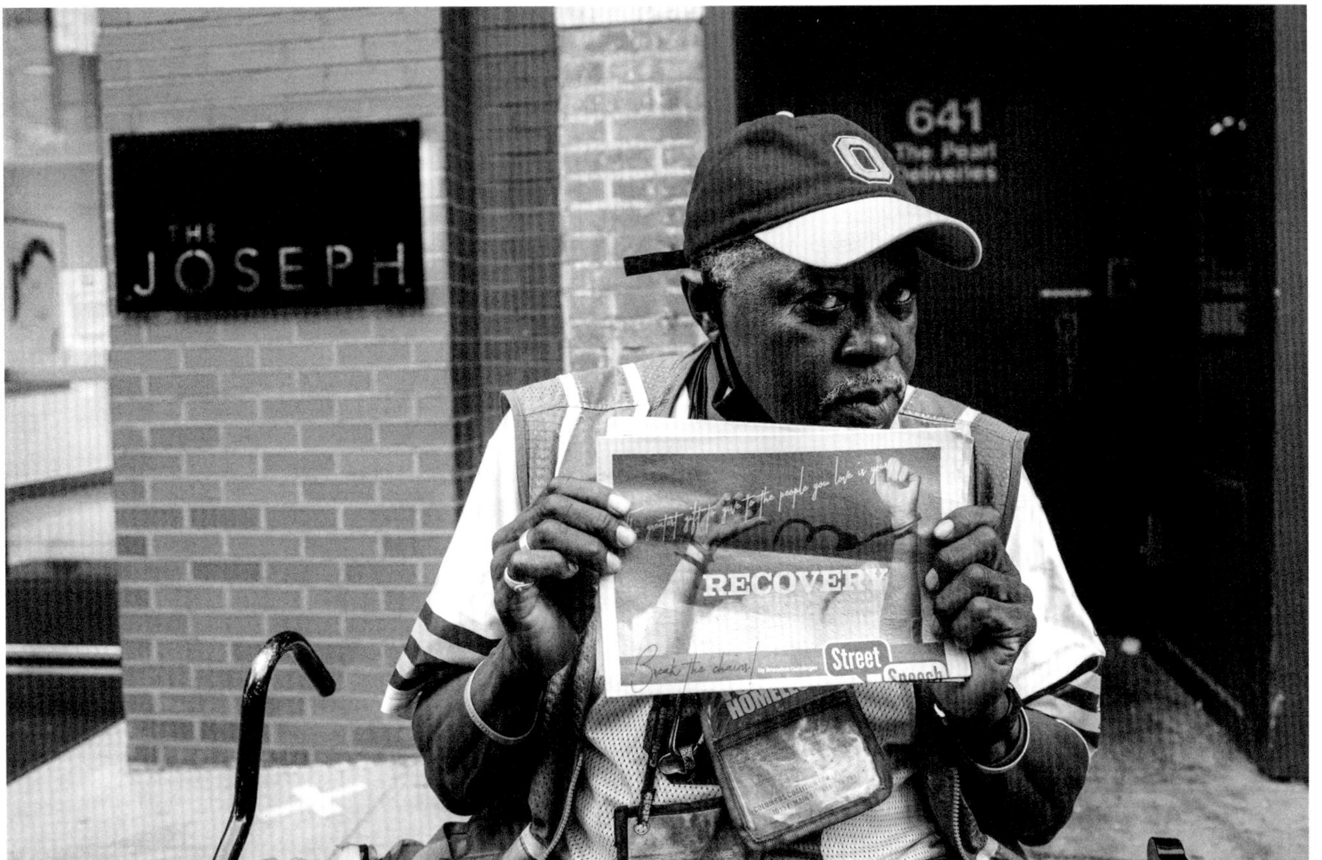

THE
JOSEPH
641
The Pearl
RECOVERY
Break the chains!
Street
Speech
HOMELESS

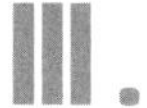

Swift Glimpse

Upon another stage of survival and recovery,
we pause and look ahead or look at each other, briefly
distrusting the resumption of the movements,
the threats, and the music of our streets.

What an empire of unequal labor, misshapen
fame, and loves whose tongues retain
the floodmarks of outswum pain.
The truthful protagonist carries a box

of brake pads, a C-clamp, and a bus pass,
or they use coupons on toothpaste and soap,
or they wash their children's clothes
while playing old songs that sound exempt

from greed, and their face, in the available light
among sidewalks, alleys, and courtyards,
can send an onlooker a swift glimpse
of the heart's unembellished excellence.

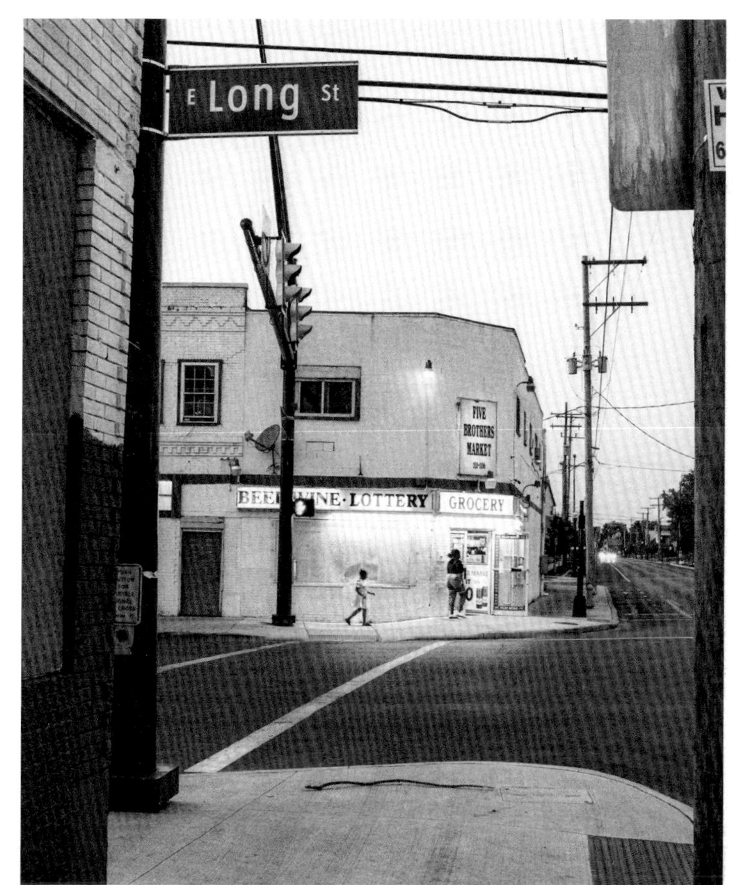
E Long St
FIVE BROTHERS MARKET
BEER WINE LOTTERY GROCERY

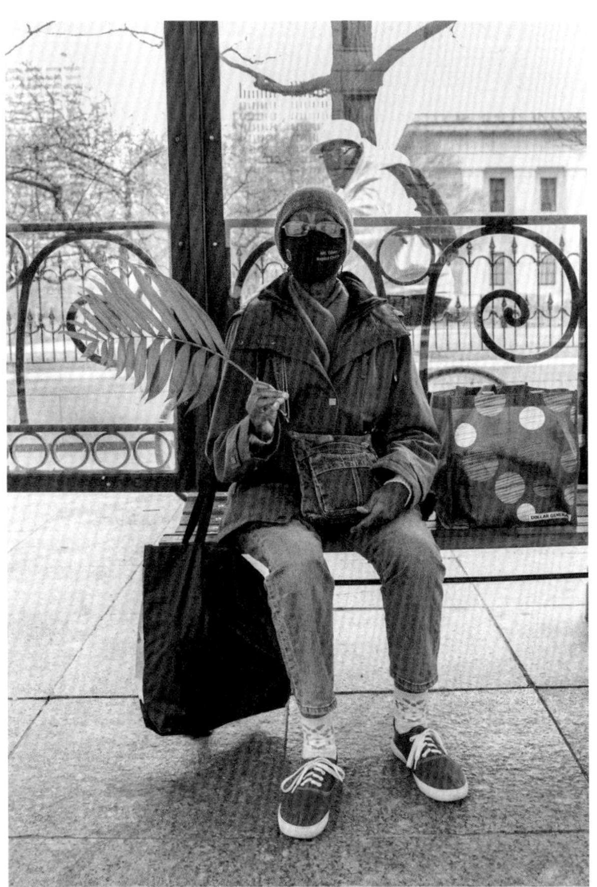

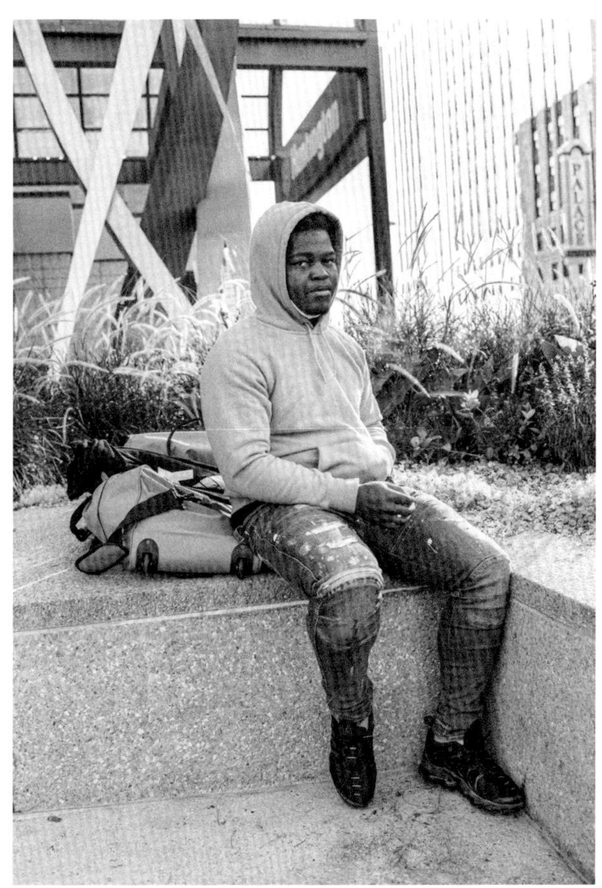

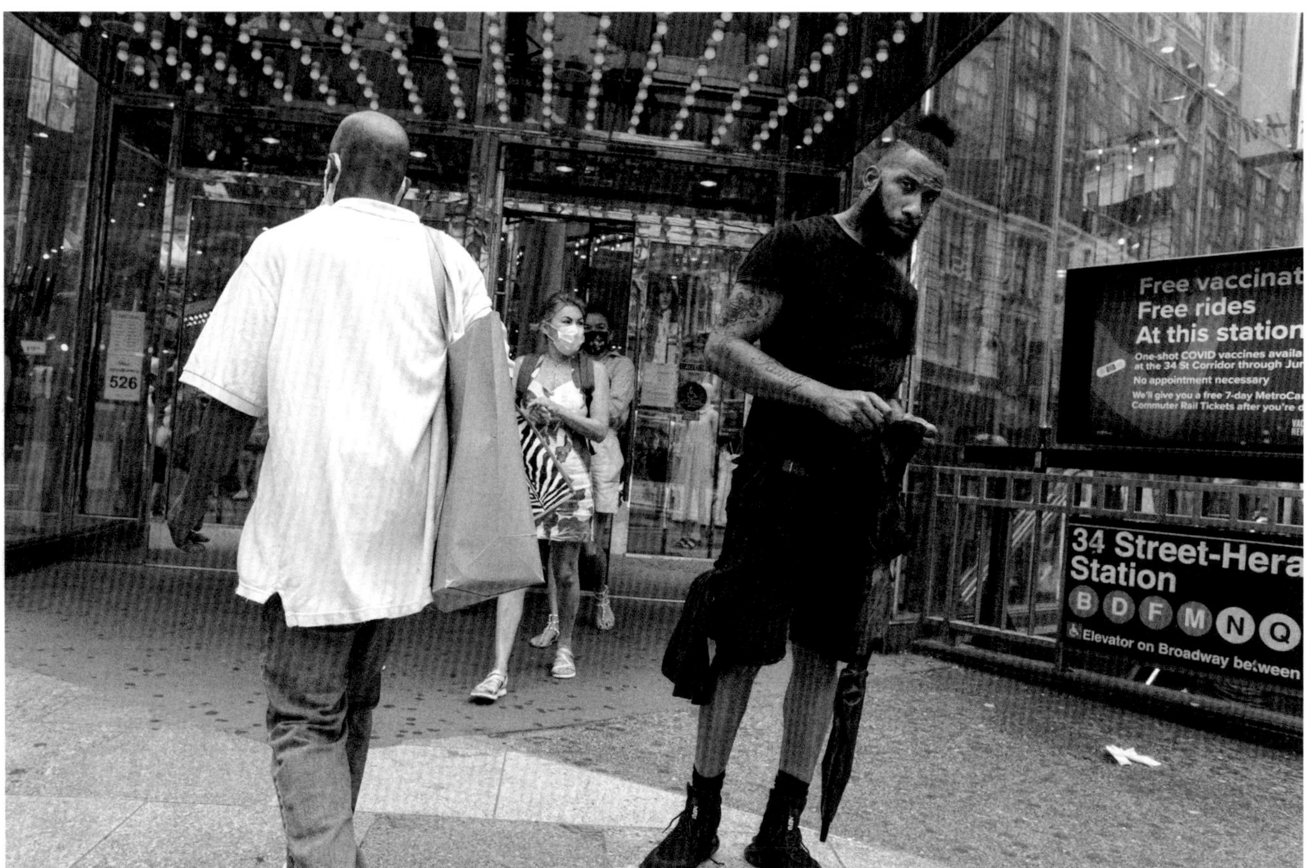
526
Free vaccinat
Free rides
At this station
One-shot COVID vaccines availa
at the 34 St Corridor through Jun
No appointment necessary
We'll give you a free 7-day MetroCar
Commuter Rail Tickets after you're d
34 Street-Hera
Station
B D F M N Q
Elevator on Broadway between

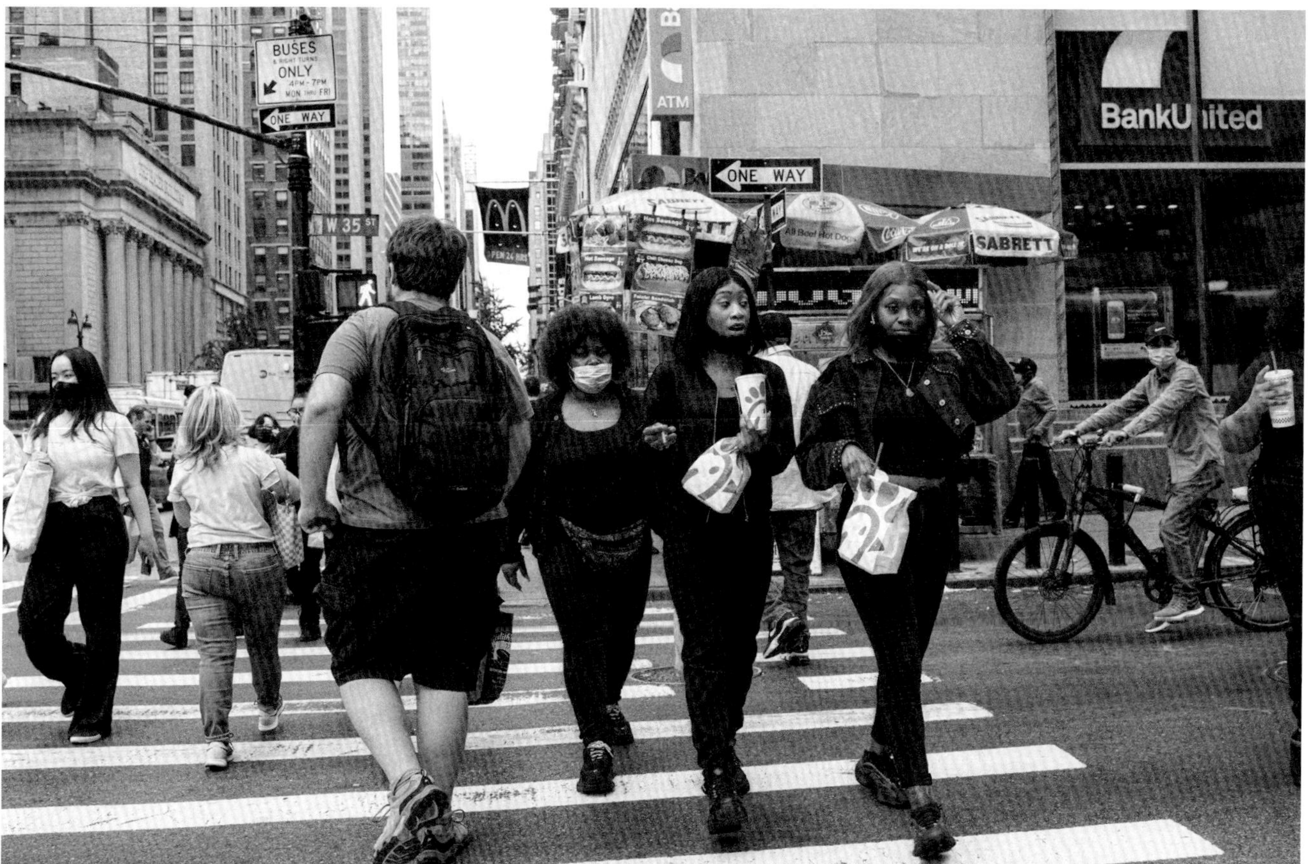

BUSES
& RIGHT TURNS
ONLY
4PM - 7PM
MON THRU FRI
ONE WAY
W 35 ST
ONE WAY
ATM
BankUnited
SABRETT
All Beef Hot Dogs

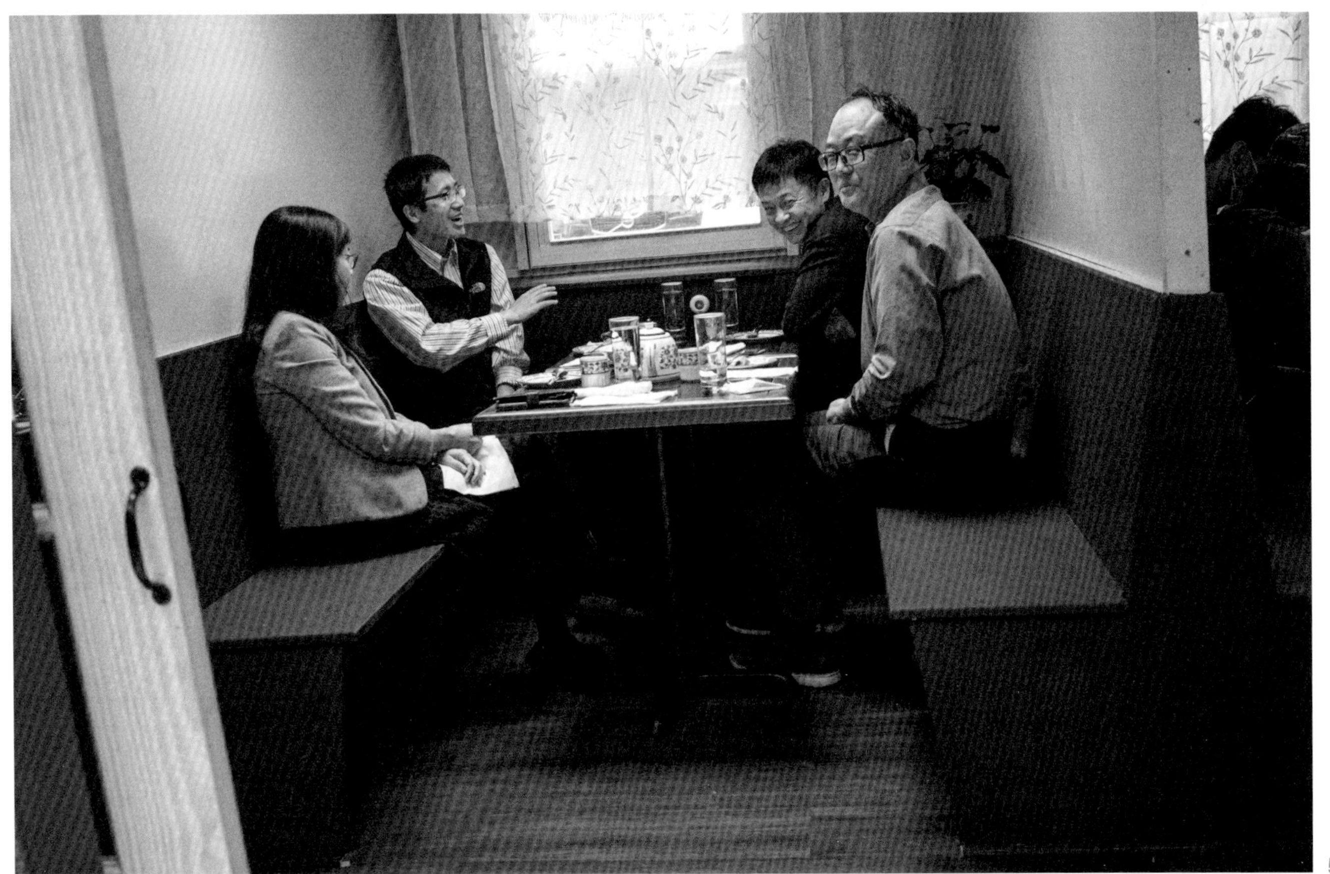

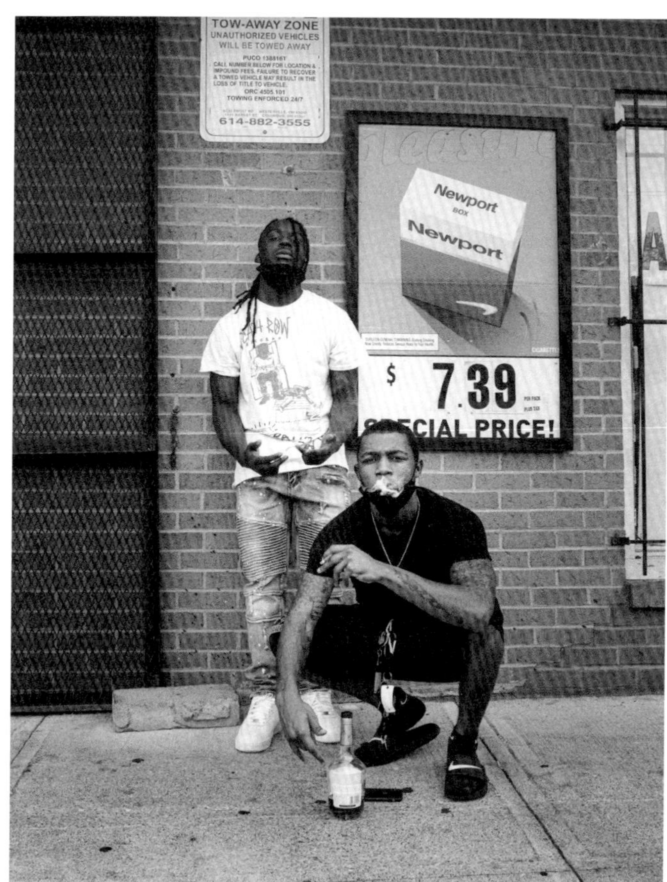
TOW-AWAY ZONE
UNAUTHORIZED VEHICLES
WILL BE TOWED AWAY
614-882-3555
Newport
BOX
Newport
$ 7.39
SPECIAL PRICE!

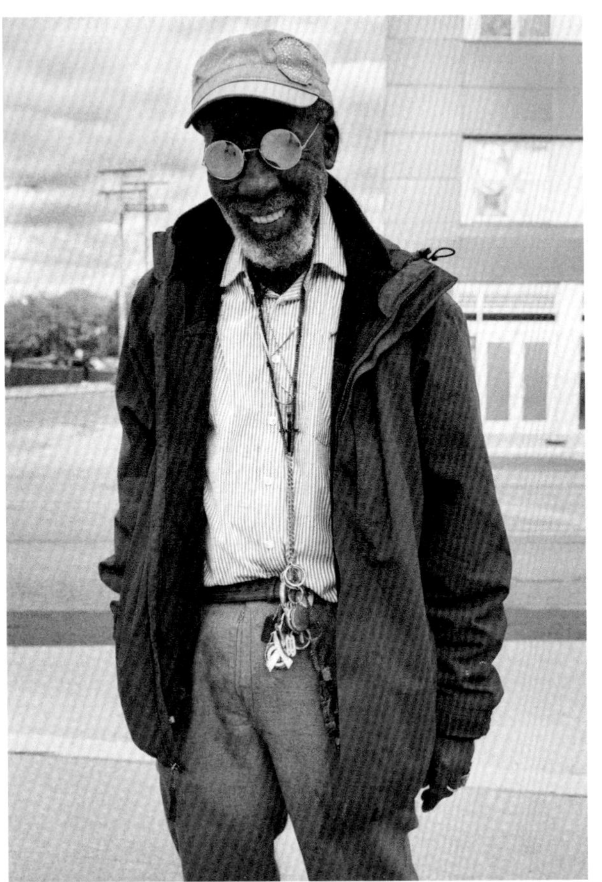

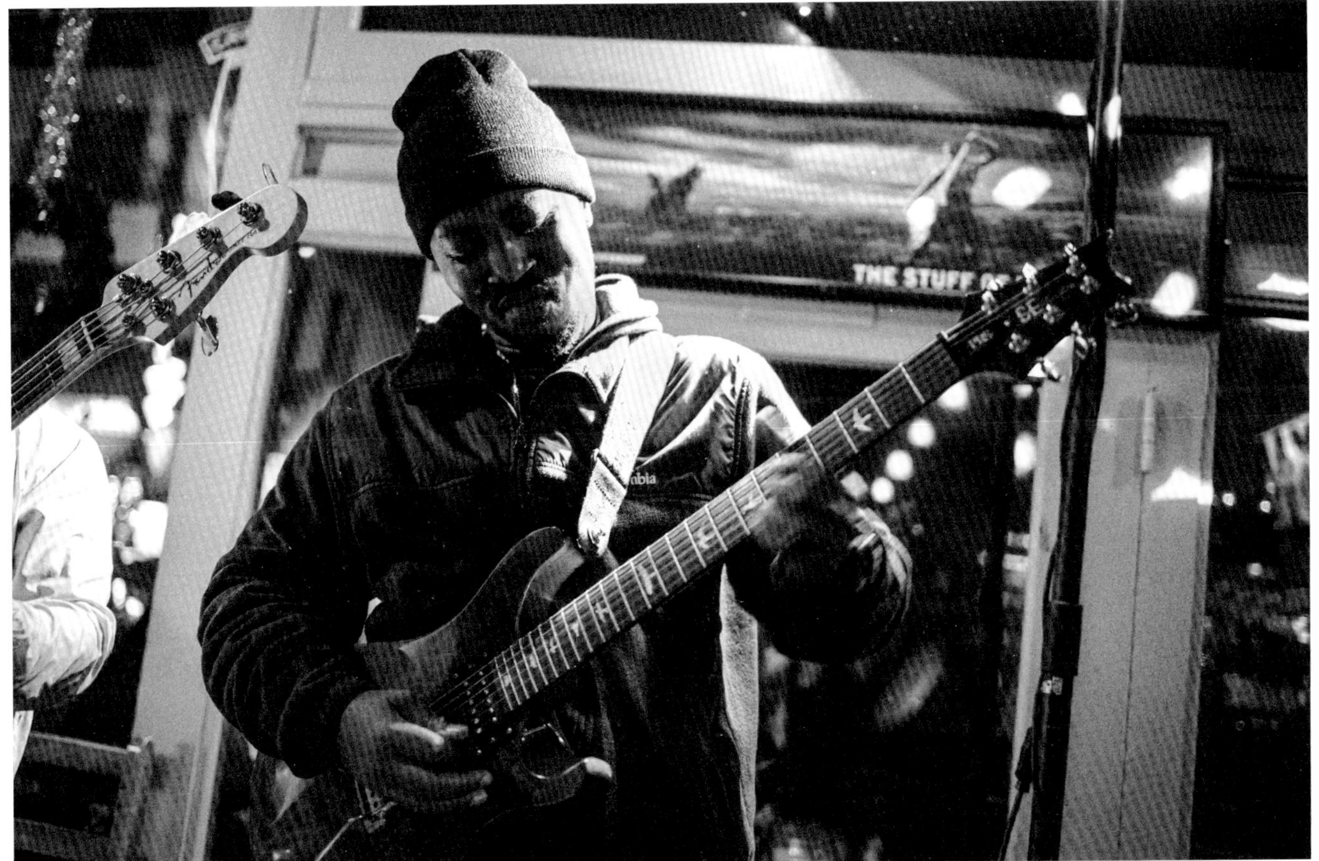

Fender
THE STUFF OF
mbia

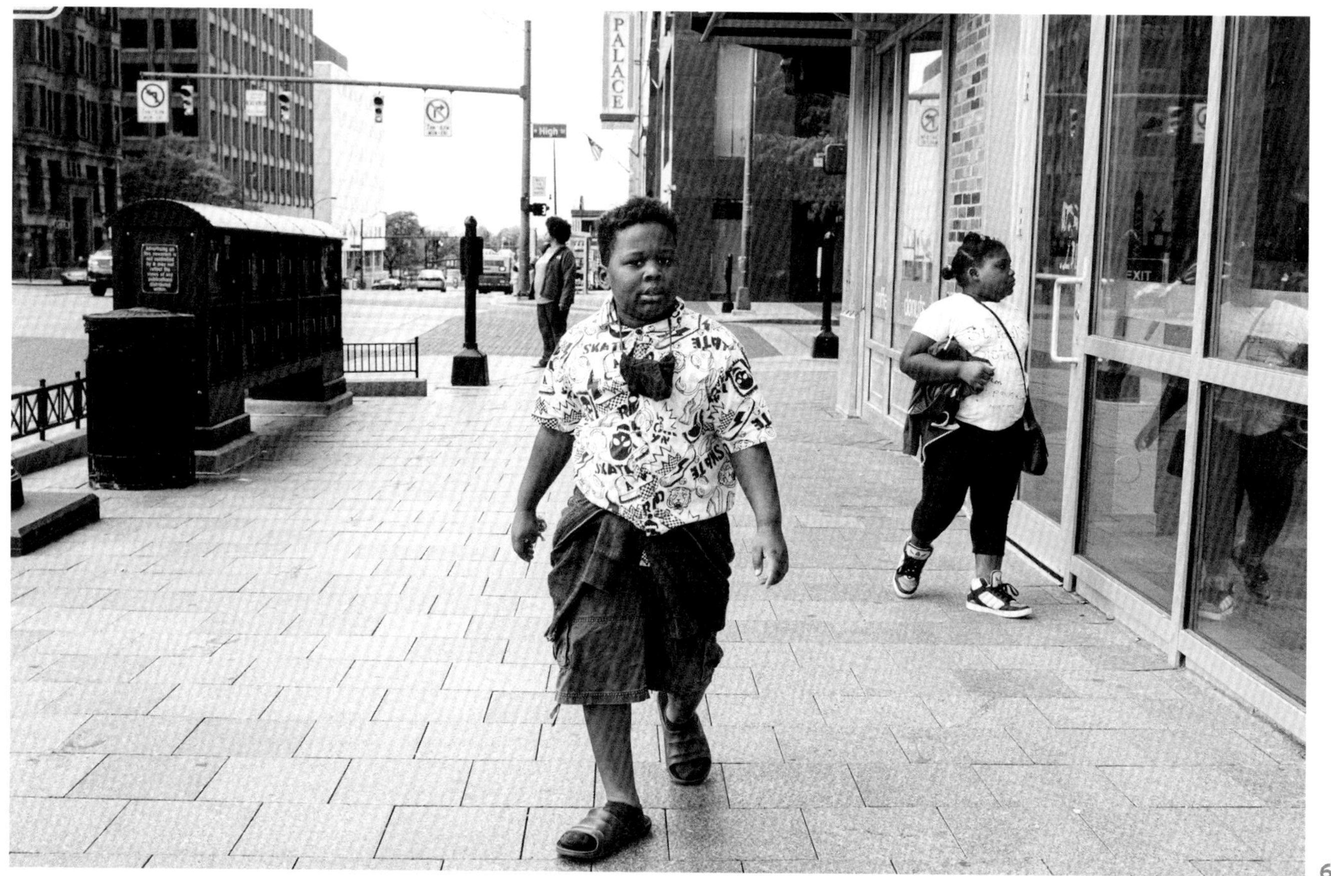

PALACE
High St
EXIT
SKATE

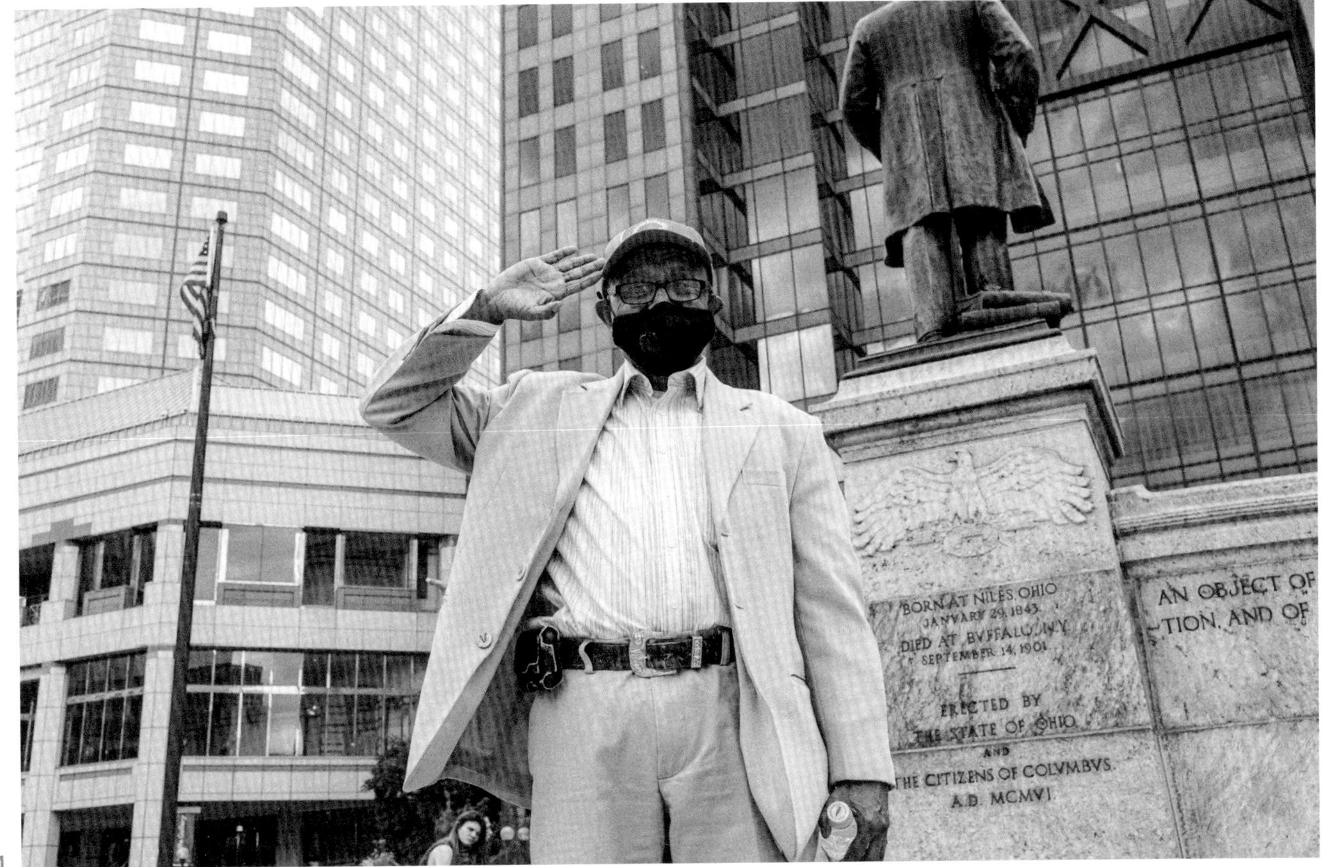

BORN AT NILES, OHIO
JANVARY 29, 1843.
DIED AT BVFFALO, N.Y.
SEPTEMBER 14, 1901.

AN OBJECT OF
TION, AND OF

ERECTED BY
THE STATE OF OHIO
AND
THE CITIZENS OF COLVMBVS.
A.D. MCMVI.

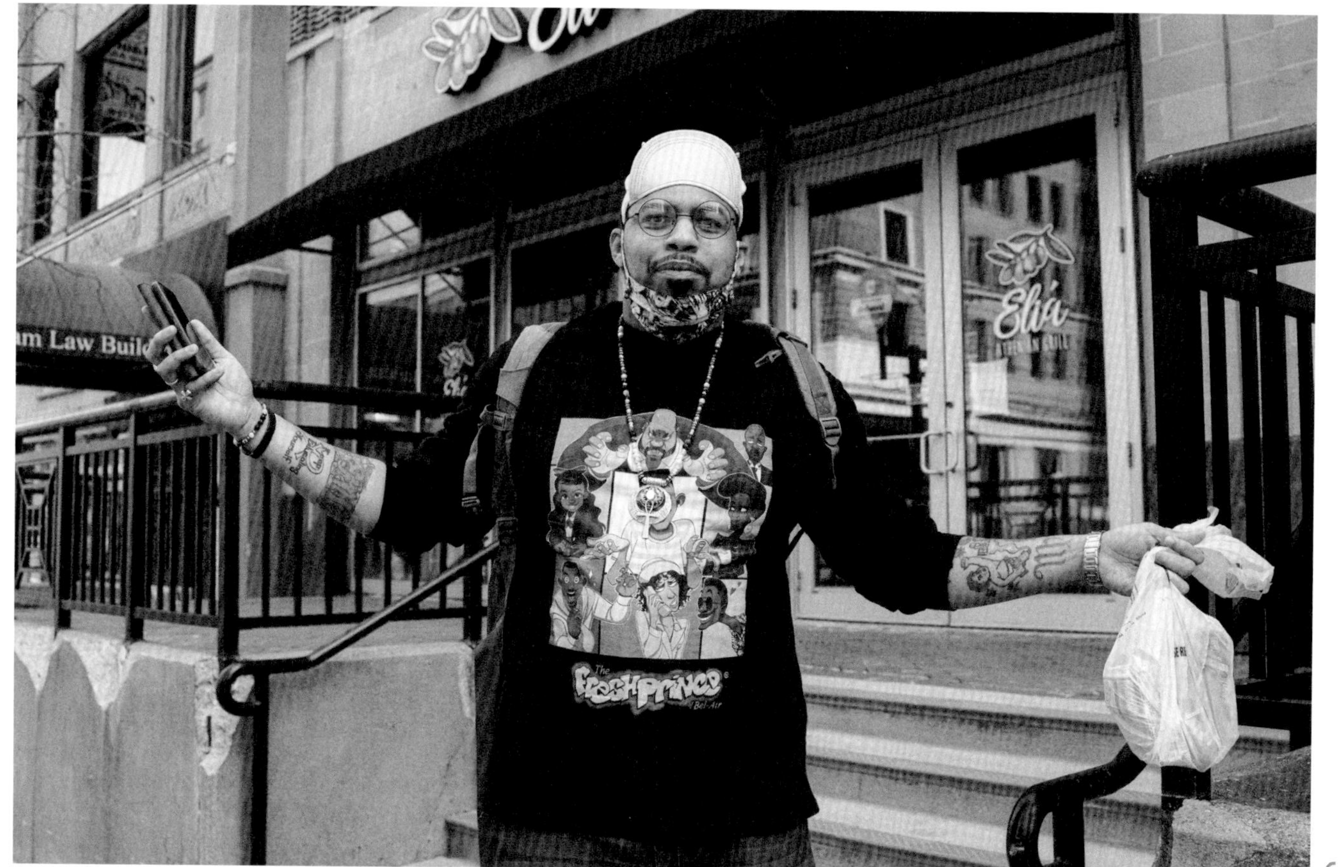

Elia
am Law Build
The FreshPrince
Bel-Air

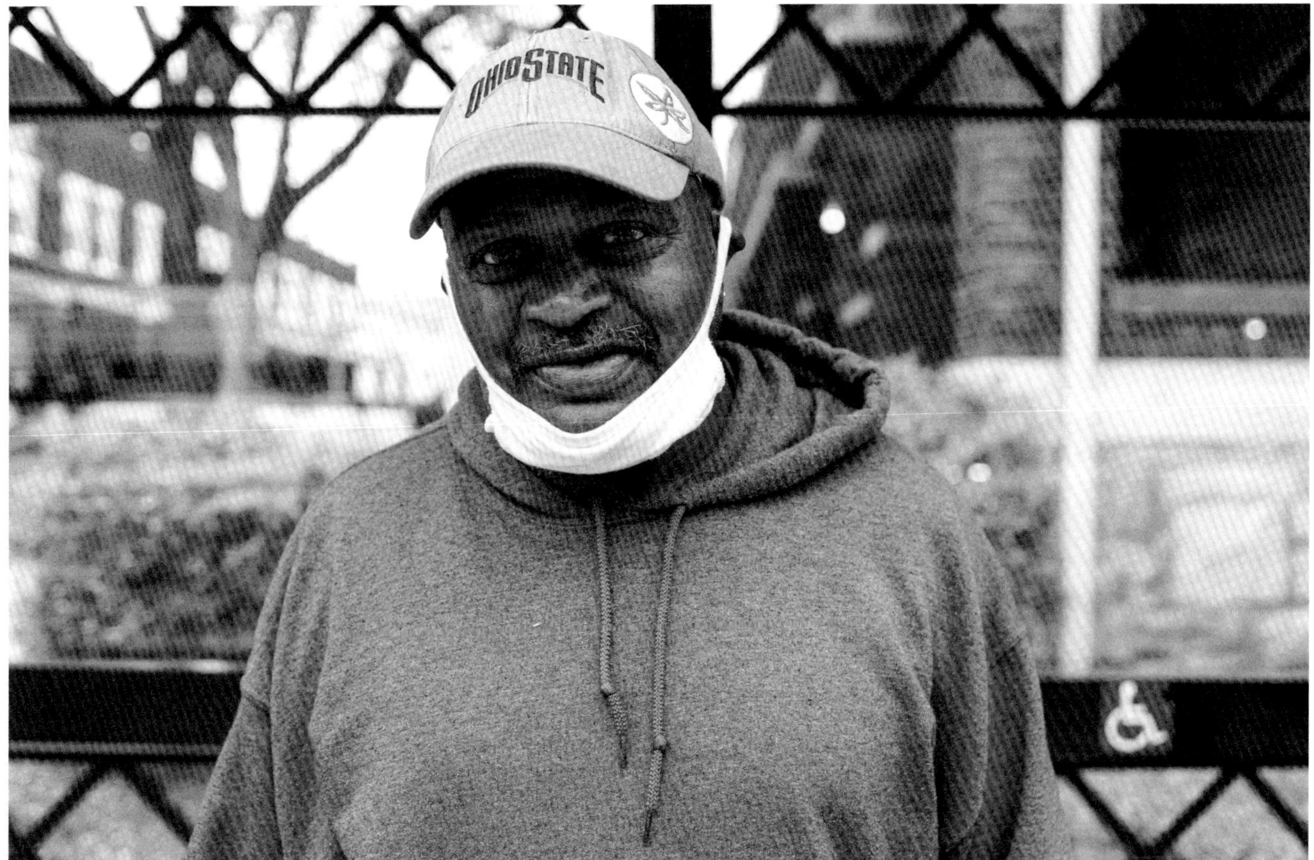
OHIO STATE

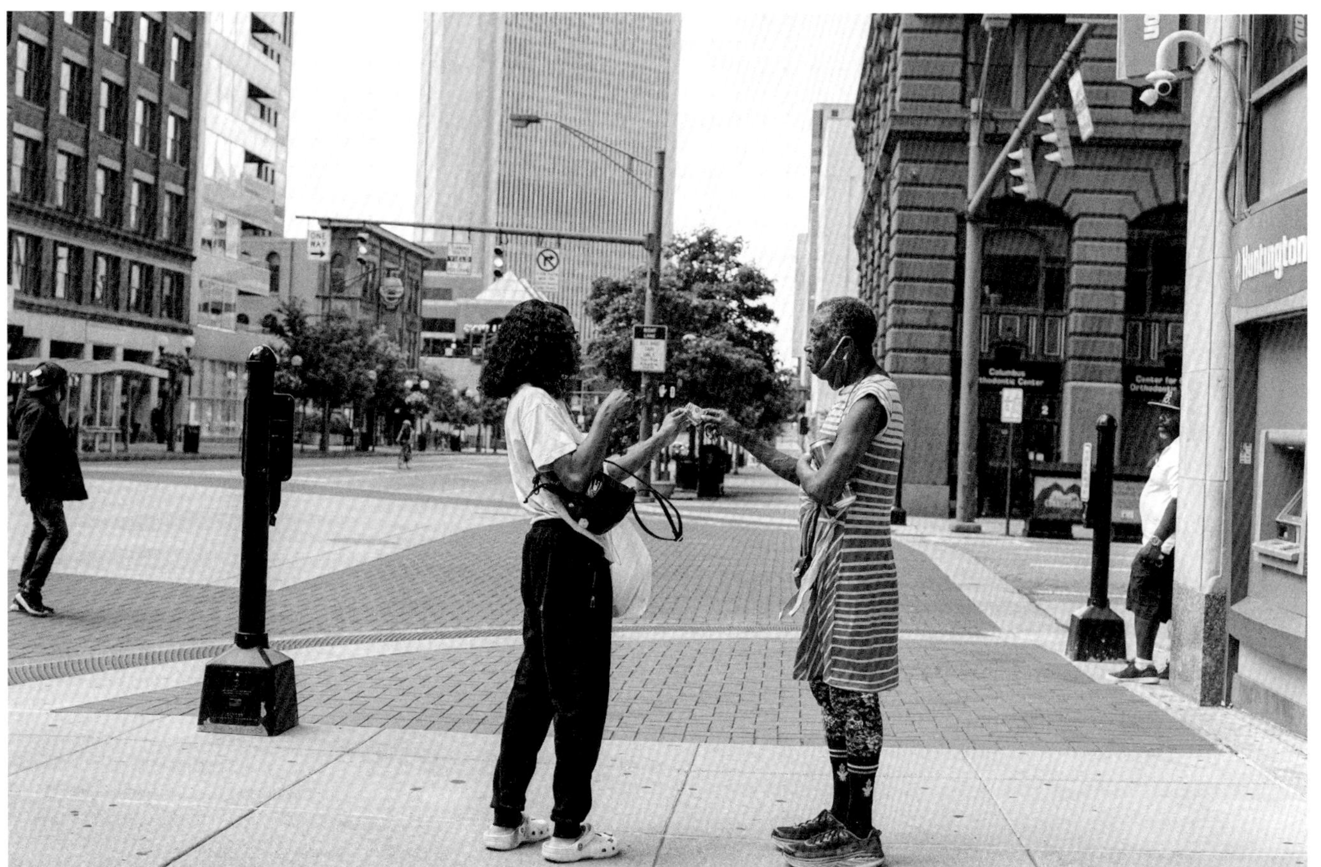

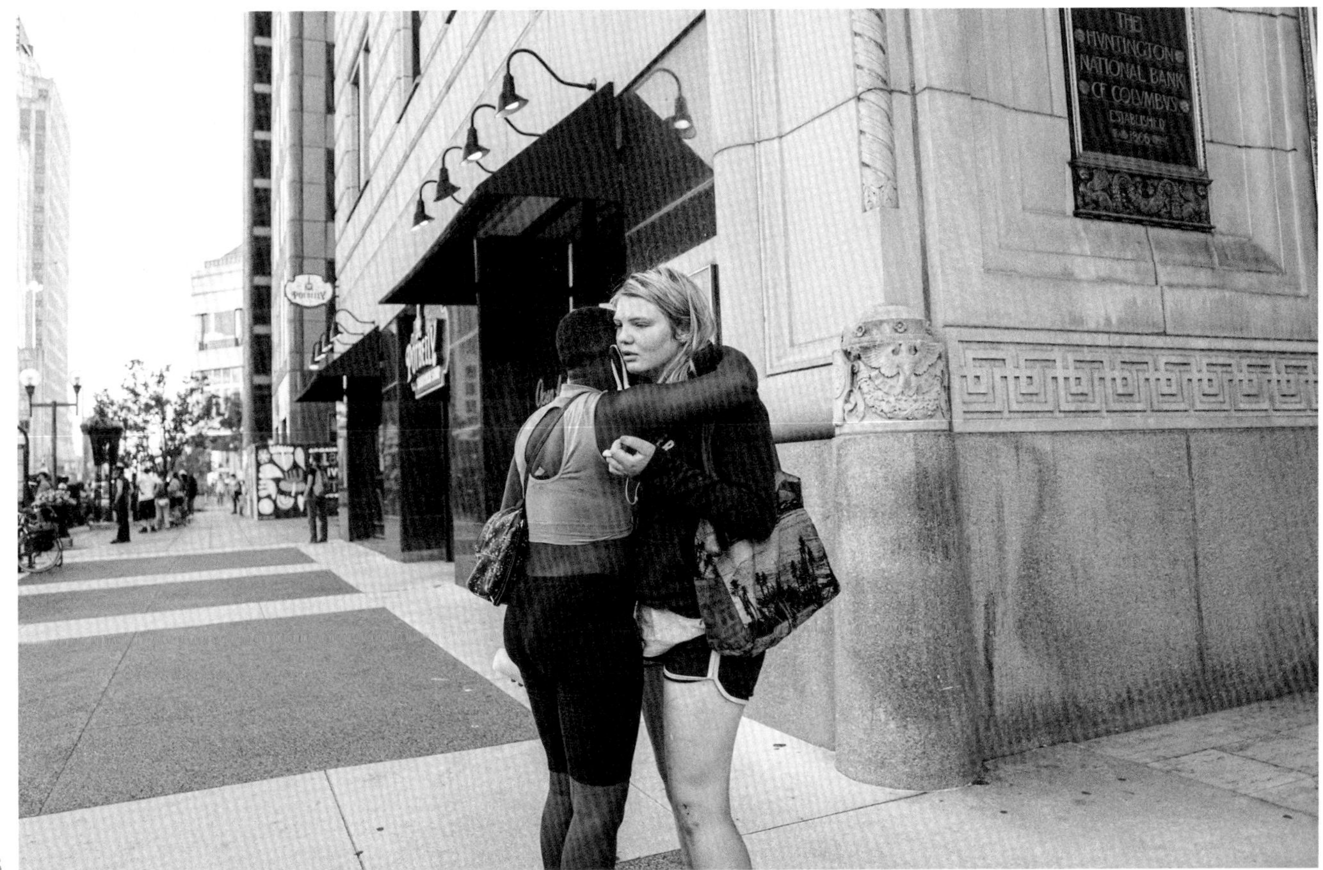

THE
HVNTINGTON
NATIONAL BANK
OF COLVMBVS
ESTABLISHED
1909

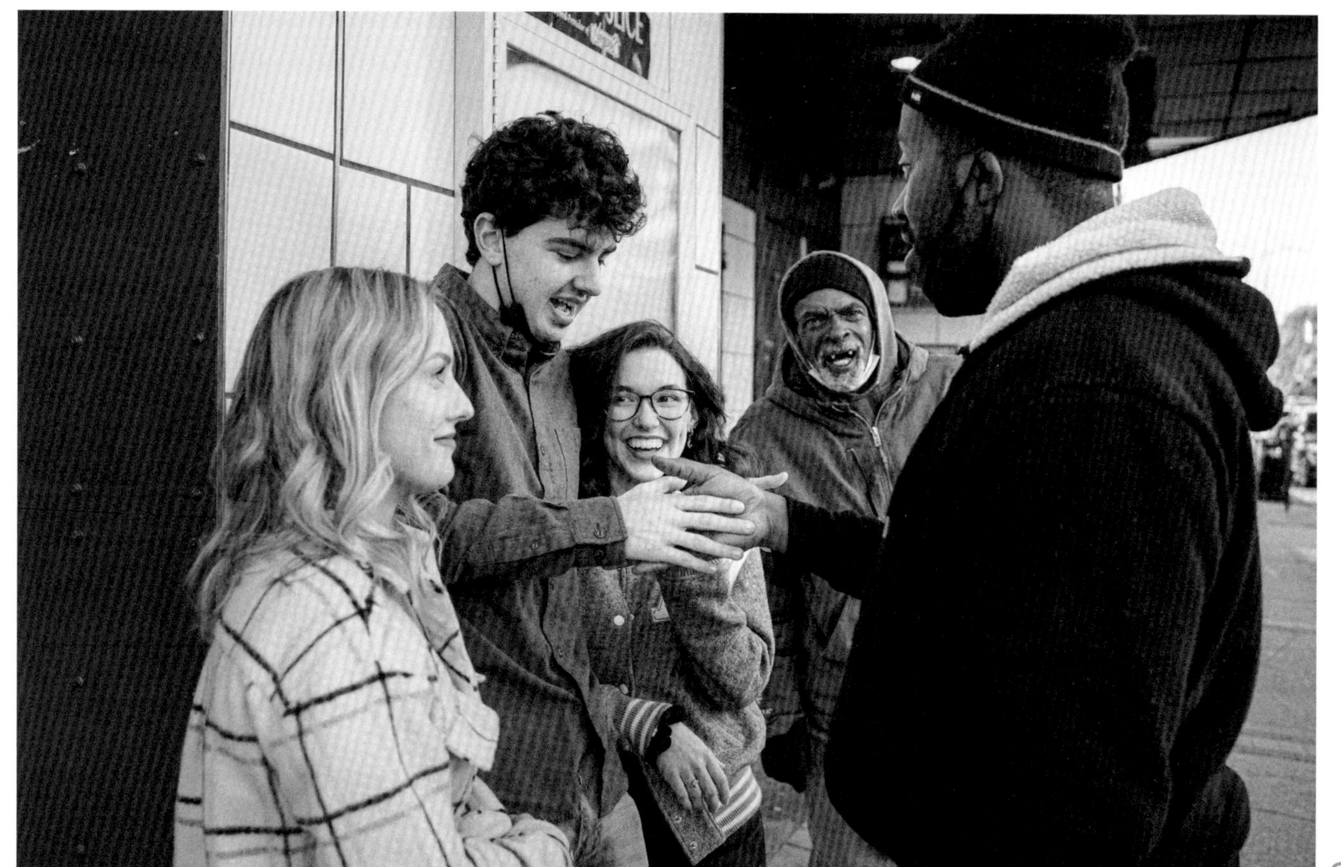

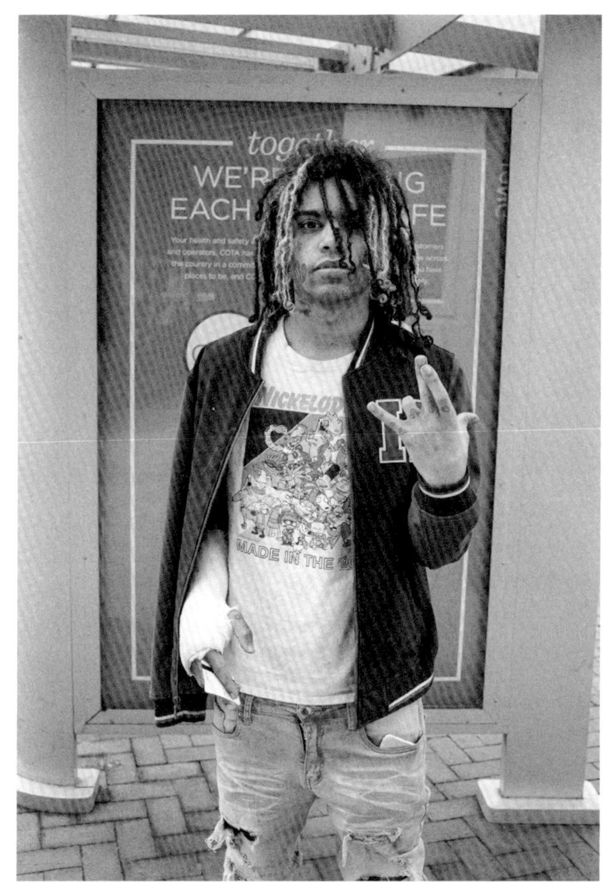

together
WE'RE ... NG
EACH ... FE

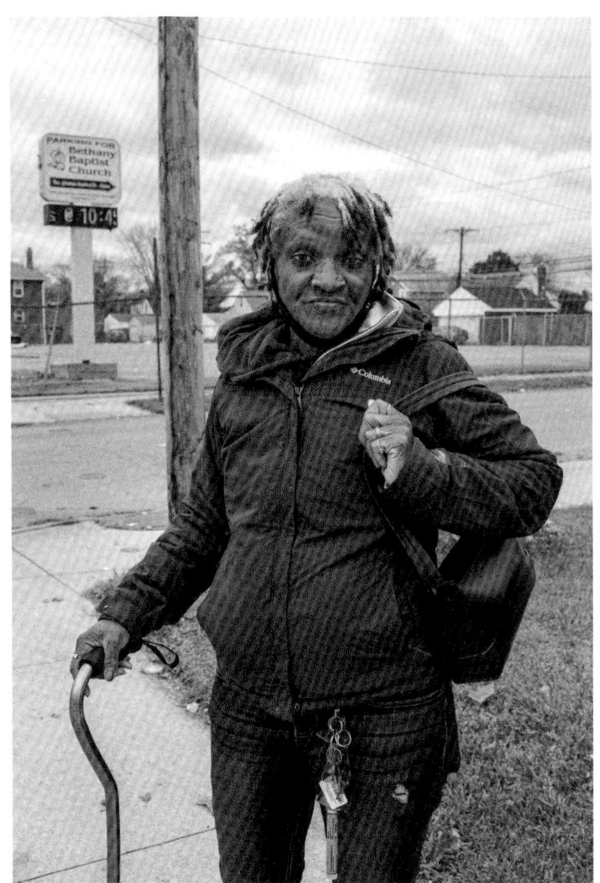
PARKING FOR
Bethany
Baptist
Church
10:4

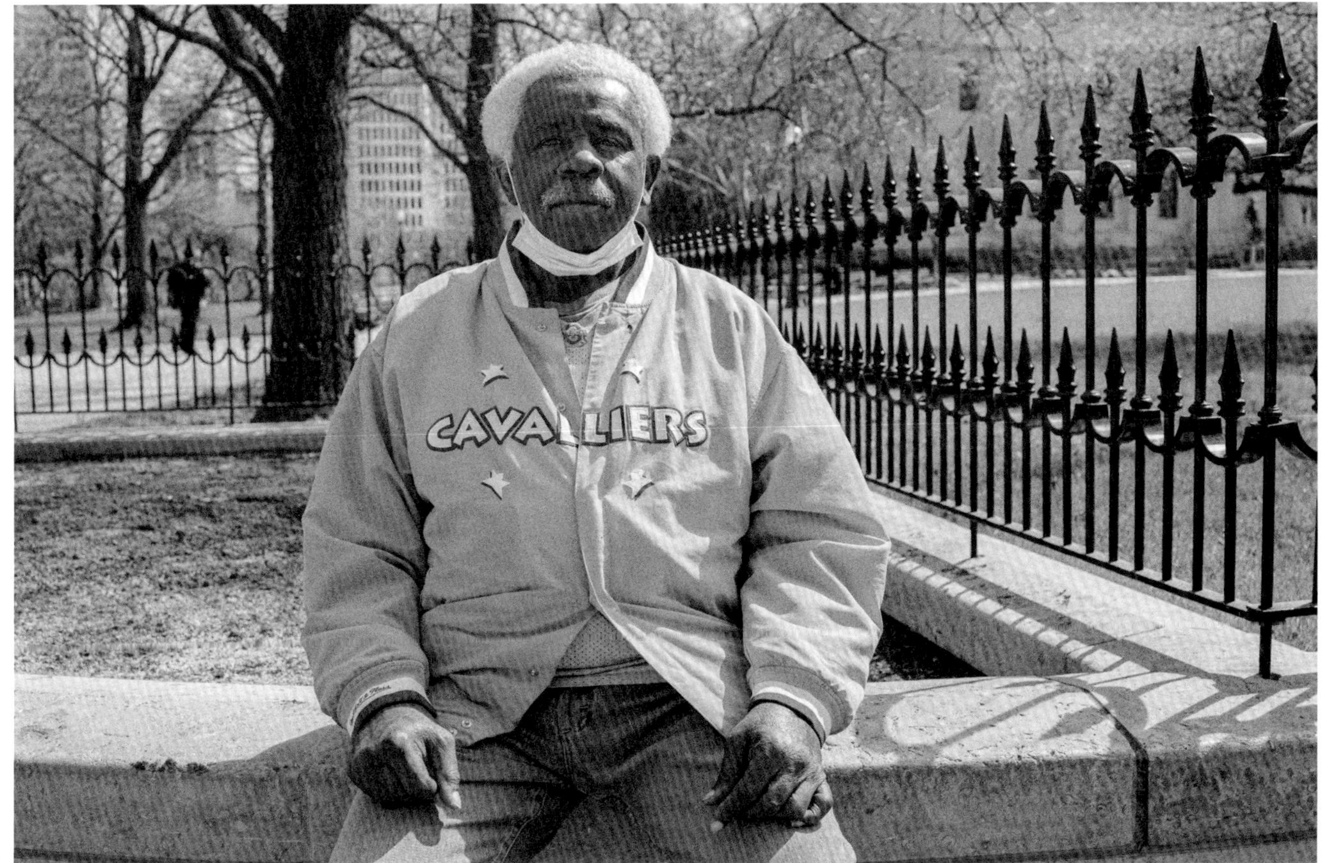
CAVALLIERS

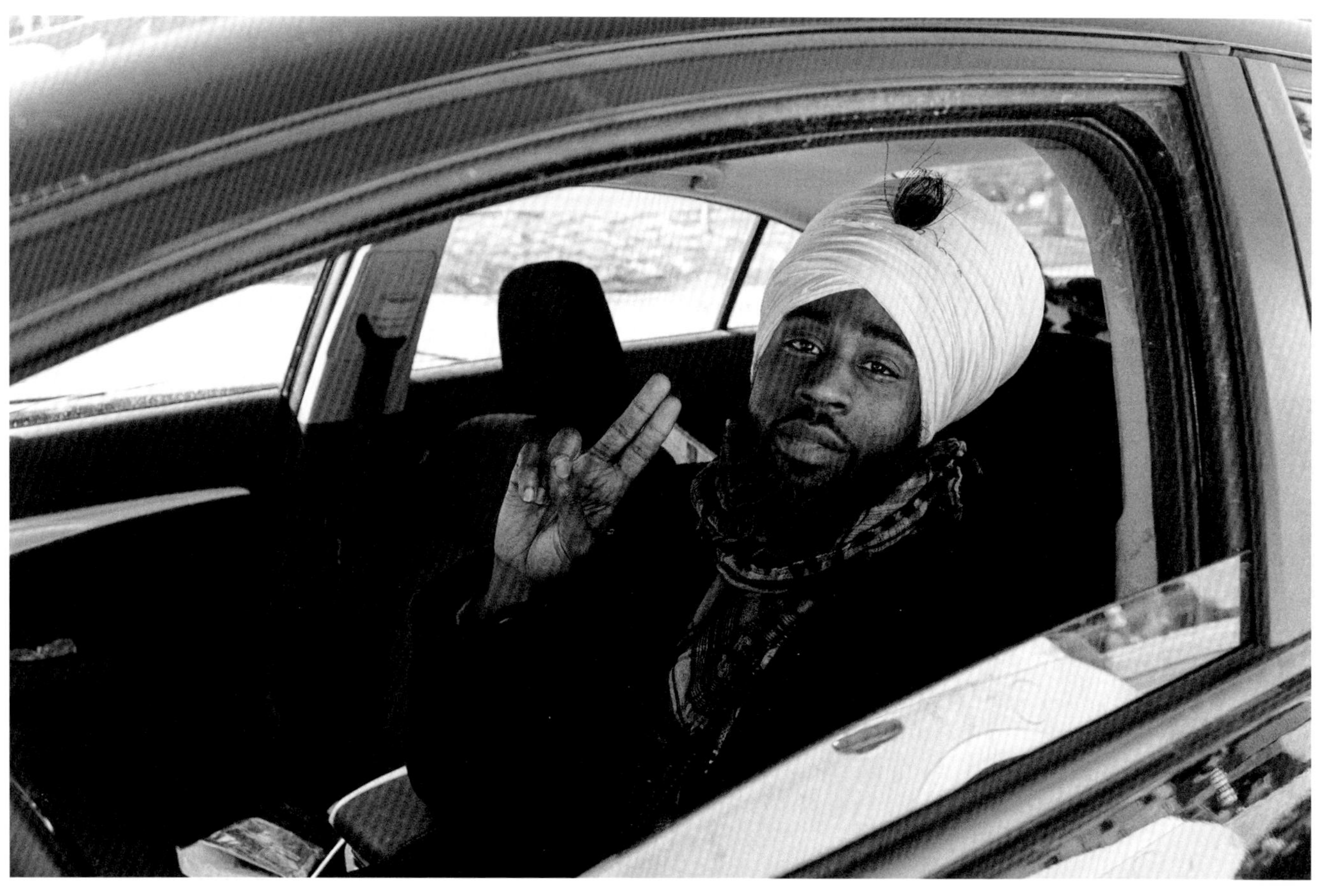

Acknowledgments

Eternal thanks to all the community members who resist peril and uplift others.

Thank you to the editors at *Action Spectacle*, *Cincinnati Review*, *Columbus Monthly*, and *Poetry* magazine for previously publishing some of this collection's photographs and poetry.

Thank you to the Greater Columbus Arts Council and the Ohio Arts Council for their unwavering support of artists across disciplines.

Notes

All photographs were made in Columbus, Toledo, or New York City, during the years 2020 and 2021.

The title of this collection is inspired by Robert Hayden's indelible 1962 poem "Those Winter Sundays," whose final lines read:

What did I know, what did I know
of love's austere and lonely offices?